OFF GRID WILDERNESS SURVIVAL MADE SIMPLE

MASTER SKILLS FOR THRIVING IN THE WOODS, DOING IT ON A BUDGET, NOT BEING SCARED AND BEING COMPLETELY INDEPENDENT FROM THE GRID

USA PROUD PUBLISHING

TABLE OF CONTENTS

INTRODUCTION

As dawn breaks, the first rays of sunlight gently kiss a landscape untamed by the modern world. You rise, not to the sound of alarms or the rush of traffic but to the serene silence of nature, punctuated by the distant call of a waking bird. You step outside, drawing a deep breath of crisp, clean air, and gaze upon a horizon unblemished by skyscrapers. This isn't just a fleeting getaway—it's your life. Every day, you relish the satisfaction of self-sufficiency and the profound peace of mind that comes from living independently, connected to the land around you. This vision of off-grid living, vibrant and fulfilling, is not just a dream; it's an attainable reality.

My journey into off-grid living was born out of necessity, curiosity, and a deep-seated passion for rediscovering our inherent ability to live in harmony with nature. After facing numerous challenges and immersing myself in both hands-on experiences and extensive research, I learned not just to survive but to thrive in the wilderness. My mission now is to share this knowledge and guide you through the transition to a lifestyle defined by self-reliance and security in the great outdoors.

In this book, I lay out clear, actionable steps and impart practical knowledge that will equip you with the confidence to prepare for and embrace off-grid living. From mastering essential survival skills to adopting sustainable living practices and understanding the psychological readiness required for such a life, I cover it all. This comprehensive guide is your roadmap to not merely surviving but flourishing off the grid.

I understand that our readers come from diverse backgrounds, each with unique motivations—be it a yearning for independence, a desire for a sustainable lifestyle, emergency preparedness, or simply the quest for a simpler, more meaningful life. Let me assure you, regardless of your reasons or current living situation, this book has something invaluable to offer you. You'll find insights and practical advice tailored to your journey toward off grid living, ensuring that you're well-equipped for this rewarding adventure.

Off Grid Wilderness Survival Made Simple: Master Skills for Thriving In The Woods, Doing It On A Budget, Not Being Scared and Being Completely Independent From The Grid is structured to guide you through every aspect of off-grid living. We start by laying the foundations, then move on to practical skills, delve into advanced survival techniques, and finally explore how to build a sustainable community. Each section builds upon the last, systematically guiding you from the planning stages to living a fully self-sufficient life.

What sets this book apart is not just the practical step-by-step instructions; it's the blend of personal anecdotes and psychological insights and a focus on community. It's about embracing the latest sustainable technologies and adopting a global perspective on what it means to live off-grid. This guide is designed to be your manual for off-grid living, complete with checklists, exercises, and actionable advice to help you make tangible progress toward your goals.

I invite you to approach this book with an open mind and a willingness to embark on one of the most rewarding journeys of your life. Engage with the exercises, reflect on your motivations, and start planning your transition with confidence and enthusiasm.

Off-grid living is more than a means to survive; it's an opportunity to thrive, reconnect with nature, and live in harmony with the environment. It's a journey that is not only possible but deeply rewarding. Let's take this first step together toward a life of independence, security, and fulfillment.

CHAPTER 1

In the symphony of modern life, where each day cascades into the next under the relentless tempo of technology and societal expectations, a question arises, subtle yet profound: What does it truly mean to be self-sufficient? This query does not echo in the void. It finds resonance in the hearts of those who seek a life unencumbered by the grid, a life where independence is not just a concept but a lived reality. Among the narratives of human endeavor, few are as compelling as the transition from dependence to autonomy. This chapter unfolds this narrative, guiding you through the psychological landscape of self-sufficiency, where the seeds of independence are sown in the fertile grounds of the mind.

THE PSYCHOLOGY OF SELF-SUFFICIENCY: CULTIVATING INDEPENDENCE

Embracing Autonomy

The human psyche, intricate and profound, harbors an innate desire for autonomy. Autonomy, the state of being self-governing, emerges not merely as a preference but as a psychological necessity for personal growth and well-being. A study published in the *Journal of Personality and Social Psychology Albert Bandura 1977* reveals that individuals who perceive a high degree of autonomy in their actions report higher levels of happiness and satisfaction. This insight sheds light on the profound impact self-reliance has on our inner world. In the context of off-grid living, embracing autonomy translates to a deliberate choice to steer away from the conventional dependencies of modern society. It's about reclaiming the narrative of your life, where each decision, from generating your own power to growing your own food, becomes a testament to your independence.

Overcoming Dependency

The transition from a life entwined with societal systems to one of self-reliance is akin to navigating uncharted waters. The initial discomfort and uncertainty are inevitable companions on this voyage. Yet, it is in the heart of the challenge that growth takes root. One effective strategy is gradual immersion. Begin by identifying one aspect of your life currently tethered to the grid— be it food, water, or energy. Research, plan, and execute a project to take this one aspect off-grid. For instance, start a small vegetable garden to reduce your reliance on commercial food sources. This approach not only fosters practical skills but also incrementally builds your confidence in your ability to live independently.

Motivation and Discipline

The path to self-sufficiency is paved with motivation and discipline. Motivation ignites the spark to pursue this lifestyle, while discipline fuels the journey. Consider the practice of journaling to maintain focus. Each morning, dedicate time to jot down your goals for the day, however small they may be. This simple act serves as a daily reminder of your purpose and progress. Furthermore, celebrate milestones, no matter their size. Completion of a project, like installing a rainwater collection system, is not just a step toward self-sufficiency but also a milestone in your personal growth journey. These celebrations reinforce your motivation, making discipline less about rigor and more about the joy of progress.

Self-Efficacy

At the core of self-sufficiency lies self-efficacy—the belief in one's ability to influence events that affect one's life. This belief is the bedrock upon which the edifice of independence is built. According to psychologist Albert Bandura, self-efficacy is developed through mastery experiences, vicarious experiences, verbal persuasion, and physiological states. In the realm of off-grid living, mastery experiences are hands-on projects that challenge your skills and expand your capabilities. Each completed project, from a successfully built composting toilet to a fully functional solar panel setup, serves as a brick in the foundation of your self-efficacy. These tangible victories not only enhance your skill set but also fortify your belief in your ability to tackle the uncertainties of off-grid living.

In conclusion, the journey to self-sufficiency is as much about cultivating the land and harnessing the elements as it is about nurturing the psyche. It demands a shift in perspective, where challenges are viewed not as obstacles but as opportunities for growth. This chapter serves as your guide through this transformative process, offering insights and strategies to foster independence, overcome dependency, maintain motivation, and build self-efficacy. As you turn these pages, remember the path to self-sufficiency begins in the mind.

THE ART OF MINIMALISM IN WILDERNESS LIVING

In the embrace of the wilderness, where the vast expanse whispers tales of simplicity and raw beauty, a revelation unfolds—true richness lies not in the abundance of possessions but in the depth of experiences. This realization paves the way for a life where minimalism isn't a mere aesthetic choice but a profound philosophy that defines every aspect of living off the grid.

At the heart of minimalism in the wilderness is the concept of freedom, liberation from the clutches of material excess. It is a deliberate paring down to the essentials, not as a sacrifice but to unburden and reclaim time and space. In this context, each item in one's life undergoes scrutiny, its presence justified only by necessity or genuine joy. This scrutiny extends beyond the physical to include activities, commitments, and even digital engagements, fostering a lifestyle marked by clarity and intention.

The line between needs and wants, often blurred by the ceaseless barrage of consumer culture, becomes stark in the wilderness. This distinction is crucial, acting as a compass guiding decisions on what to bring into one's life. A need, in its purest form, sustains life or significantly enhances well-being, such as shelter, nutritious food, and clean water. Wants, while they can add comfort or pleasure, are not vital for survival or happiness. Recognizing this difference is not an innate skill but one honed through mindful practice and reflection. One practical approach is the "use it or lose it" method, where items not used within a specific timeframe are reevaluated for their necessity, encouraging a cycle of conscious consumption and release.

Mindful consumption emerges as a natural extension of this practice, a choice to prefer sustainability over convenience. This choice manifests in various forms, from selecting durable goods over disposable ones to embracing renewable energy sources. It signifies a shift from passive consumption to active participation in the life cycle of products, understanding their origin, impact, and end-of-life. Mindful consumption in the wilderness is not about deprivation but about making informed decisions that align with the values of self-sufficiency and environmental stewardship. For instance, choosing to repair a tool rather than replace it not only saves resources but also deepens one's connection to one's possessions, imbuing them with personal history and meaning.

Space and efficiency become paramount in wilderness living, where the confines of a shelter demand ingenious solutions to maximize both functionality and comfort. This necessity breeds innovation, turning constraints into a canvas for creativity. Organizing living spaces in the wilderness is an exercise in efficiency, where every item has its place, and multifunctionality is prized. Furniture that doubles as storage, vertical gardening, and foldable designs are examples of how space can be optimized without compromising quality of life. Moreover, this focus on efficiency extends to the layout of the living area itself, designed to harmonize with natural elements to enhance heating, cooling, and lighting, further reducing the need for external resources.

In practicing the art of minimalism in wilderness living, one finds that the true essence of home is not in the abundance of possessions but in the quality of the space to inspire, heal, and connect. It is a space where simplicity reigns, free from the clutter that clouds the mind, allowing one to live with a sense of purpose and presence. This minimalist approach is not just about physical space; it is a mindset that permeates every aspect of life, encouraging a deeper appreciation for the natural world and fostering a lifestyle that is sustainable, intentional, and profoundly fulfilling.

Through the lens of minimalism, wilderness living transforms from a challenge to be conquered into a dialogue with nature, where each decision, each simplification, brings one closer to the essence of being. It is a testament to the power of less, a reminder that in the absence of excess, we find room for growth, creativity, and a peace that transcends material. In this way, minimalism becomes not just a practice but a path to freedom, a journey toward a life lived with depth, purpose, and harmony with the natural world.

RESILIENCE TRAINING: PREPARING YOUR MIND FOR THE UNPREDICTABLE

In the vast canvas of wilderness living, unpredictability paints its strokes with broad and often unexpected swipes. Resilience, then, becomes not just a trait to aspire to but a necessity for survival. This resilience is multifaceted, encompassing the ability to adapt, manage stress, solve problems creatively, and draw on the strength of a community.

Adaptability in the face of change and unforeseen challenges emerges as a cornerstone of resilience. It requires a mindset that views change not as a threat but as an integral part of the natural cycle, an opportunity for growth. To cultivate this adaptability, one might practice scenario planning, a technique where you envision various potential challenges and outline practical responses. For instance, if a sudden storm were to disrupt your water supply, having multiple contingency plans in place ensures you're not left vulnerable. This mental exercise not only prepares you for specific scenarios but also trains your mind to think flexibly and react calmly to any situation.

Emotional resilience, the capacity to navigate the turbulent waters of stress and maintain a buoyant spirit, is another critical component. This resilience is nurtured through practices that anchor the mind—such as meditation, which teaches the art of observing thoughts without getting swept away by them. Another powerful tool is the practice of gratitude. By maintaining a journal to recount daily moments of thankfulness, you reinforce a positive outlook, which acts as a buffer against the corrosive effects of stress. This habit of seeking out and appreciating the good, even during hardship, fosters a resilient mindset that can withstand the pressures of off-grid living.

Problem-solving, the ability to confront obstacles with a clear head and creative solutions, is essential in an environment where traditional resources and support systems may be absent. Enhancing these skills involves cultivating a mindset of curiosity and openness to learning. For example, when faced with a malfunctioning solar panel, instead of yielding to frustration, approach the problem with curiosity. Research, experimentation, and perhaps consultation with more knowledgeable individuals turn the situation into a learning opportunity. This approach not only solves the immediate problem but also expands your knowledge base and skill set for future challenges.

Community support stands as a pillar of resilience, offering a network of knowledge, experience, and emotional backing. In the off-grid context, this support takes on heightened significance. Building relationships with neighbors and local communities creates a safety net of mutual assistance. Workshops, skill shares, and regular community meetings foster a sense of belonging and collective strength. Moreover, online forums dedicated to off-grid living can provide invaluable insights and encouragement from those who have navigated similar paths. This interconnected web of support ensures that when challenges arise, you're not facing them alone but are buoyed by the collective wisdom and strength of a community.

In weaving these threads of resilience—adaptability, emotional fortitude, problem-solving acumen, and community support—you prepare not just for the practicalities of off-grid living but for a life rich in learning and growth. Through this preparation, the unpredictable becomes not a source of fear but a landscape of possibilities, where each challenge is an opportunity to deepen your resilience and expand your capabilities.

SUSTAINABLE LIVING: ENVIRONMENTAL STEWARDSHIP AS A PILLAR

In the realm of off-grid existence, where the rhythms of nature dictate the ebb and flow of daily life, a deep-seated respect for the environment emerges not as an optional ethos but as a foundational principle. This respect manifests through a series of deliberate, eco-conscious choices that ripple through every facet of living, from the procurement of resources to the disposal of waste. It is within this context that sustainability transcends the realm of a buzzword to become a tangible expression of one's commitment to environmental stewardship.

At the heart of these eco-conscious choices lies the imperative to minimize one's ecological footprint, a concept that comprehends the full spectrum of human impact on the environment. This imperative guides decisions both large and small, from the selection of materials for building an off-grid home to the daily consumption of water and energy. For instance, opting for locally sourced, sustainably harvested timber not only reduces the carbon emissions associated with transportation but also supports local ecosystems and economies. Similarly, the choice to consume less water, perhaps by installing low-flow fixtures or adopting water-wise gardening techniques, reflects a broader commitment to preserving precious natural resources.

The utilization of renewable resources stands as a cornerstone of sustainable off-grid living, offering a path to energy independence that harmonizes with the principles of environmental stewardship. Solar panels that capture the sun's rays, wind turbines that dance with the breeze, and micro-hydro systems that harness the power of flowing water embody the transition from passive consumers of energy to active participants in the generation of power. These systems, rooted in the inexhaustible bounty of nature, offer not only a sustainable alternative to fossil fuels but also a profound sense of connection to the natural world. The sun's daily journey across the sky, the changing patterns of the wind, and the rhythmic flow of water become not just meteorological phenomena but integral aspects of one's energy landscape.

Biodiversity, the rich tapestry of life that sustains ecosystems, emerges as a critical consideration in the design and management of off-grid spaces. The importance of maintaining biodiversity extends beyond the aesthetic or sentimental; it encompasses the vital ecological services that diverse species provide, from pollination and pest control to soil health and water purification. In practice, fostering biodiversity might involve the creation of wildlife habitats, the planting of native species, or the restoration of natural waterways. These actions not only enhance the resilience and productivity of one's off-grid homestead but also contribute to the broader health of the planet. Moreover, living near a diverse array of flora and fauna serves as a daily reminder of the interconnectedness of all life, reinforcing the ethos of environmental stewardship that underpins sustainable off-grid living.

Waste reduction, a principle that challenges the throwaway culture of modern society, becomes a practical and philosophical imperative in the off-grid context. Strategies for reducing, reusing, and recycling waste permeate every aspect of daily life, from the kitchen to the workshop. Composting organic waste, for instance, transforms what might otherwise be seen as refuse into a valuable resource that nourishes the soil and supports plant growth. Similarly, repurposing materials, whether it's turning pallets into furniture or reusing glass jars for storage, reflects a commitment to viewing waste not as an inevitable byproduct of living but as a resource to be creatively and responsibly managed. This approach to waste reduction not only minimizes the impact on landfills and reduces the demand for new materials but also cultivates a mindset of resourcefulness and appreciation for the value inherent in all materials.

In the tapestry of sustainable off-grid living, each thread—from eco-conscious choices and the utilization of renewable resources to the preservation of biodiversity and the reduction of waste— weaves together to create a fabric of environmental stewardship that is both resilient and beautiful. This fabric, rich with the colors of commitment, innovation, and respect, drapes the landscape of off-grid living, offering shelter and sustenance not just for those who dwell within but for the planet that sustains us all. Through this lens, sustainability becomes not just a series of practices but a way of being, a deep-seated ethos that informs every decision and shapes every action. It is a manifestation of the belief that to live off the grid is to live in harmony with the earth, to take only what is needed and to give back in equal measure, to honor the cycles of nature, and to protect the delicate balance that sustains all life. In this way, sustainable off-grid living becomes a powerful expression of environmental stewardship, a testament to the possibility of a life that is not only self-sufficient but also deeply interconnected with the natural world.

THE EVOLUTION OF THE OFF-GRID MOVEMENT: A HISTORICAL PERSPECTIVE

In tracing the lineage of the off-grid ethos, one uncovers a narrative not merely of survival but of profound human adaptability and ingenuity. The concept of self-sufficiency, while appearing as a contemporary counter-narrative to grid-tied existence, roots itself deeply in the annals of human history. From the indigenous tribes whose lives flowed in harmony with the land to the homesteaders of the nineteenth century who carved out lives of autonomy in the wilderness, the desire to live in a manner that is directly connected to and respectful of the earth's rhythms has been a persistent human endeavor.

This legacy of self-reliance, however, was not merely a matter of choice but a necessity. As societies evolved, so did the complexity of living independently from the burgeoning infrastructures that sought to bind communities into an interconnected web of dependence. Yet, even as the twentieth century heralded an era of unprecedented technological growth and urbanization, a countermovement quietly germinated, drawing individuals and communities back toward the ideals of self-sufficiency and environmental stewardship.

The technological leaps that characterized the late twentieth and early twenty-first centuries served as a double-edged sword in the narrative of off-grid living. On the one hand, advancements in solar panel efficiency, wind turbine technology, and water purification systems have dismantled many of the barriers that once made off-grid living a formidable challenge. These innovations, coupled with the advent of the internet, have democratized access to information, allowing aspiring off-gridders to learn, connect, and share knowledge on a global scale. The tools and technologies that once tethered individuals to the grid have been reimagined, enabling a life of autonomy that does not forsake the conveniences of modernity but redefines them within the parameters of sustainability and self-reliance.

On the other hand, the proliferation of technology has catalyzed a cultural reevaluation of what it means to live a fulfilled life. The relentless pace of digital consumption and the growing disillusionment with the ecological and social ramifications of unchecked industrial growth has prompted a collective introspection. In this milieu, off-grid living emerges not as a retreat from society but as a critique of and an alternative to the prevailing models of consumption and existence. This shift reflects a broader cultural awakening to the values of minimalism, sustainability, and community, values that are intrinsic to the off-grid ethos.

The pioneers of the contemporary off-grid movement, individuals, and communities who have navigated the transition from grid dependency to self-sufficiency stand as testaments to the viability of this lifestyle. Their stories, diverse in geography and context, share a common thread of resilience, innovation, and a deep-seated respect for the natural world. These pioneers have not only charted a course for those who follow but also contributed to the evolution of the off-grid movement through their experiments, successes, and even their failures.

In regions where the grid was either inaccessible or unreliable, off-grid living has been a long-standing practice out of necessity. However, the intentional choice to live off-grid, motivated by ecological concerns, a desire for independence, or both, has seen a significant uptick in recent years. This trend is not confined to remote wilderness areas but is evident in suburban and urban settings, where rooftop gardens, solar panels, and rainwater harvesting systems signal a shift toward more sustainable, autonomous ways of living.

Moreover, the off-grid movement has inspired a renaissance of traditional skills and knowledge, from permaculture and natural building techniques to foraging and herbal medicine. This revival of ancient wisdom, integrated with modern technology and ecological science, has enriched the off-grid lifestyle, making it not only a viable alternative to conventional living but also a dynamic field of innovation and learning.

As this movement has grown, so too has the recognition of the need for legal and societal frameworks that support and facilitate off-grid living. Advocacy and dialogue with policymakers have led to changes in zoning laws, building codes, and energy regulations in some areas, reflecting a growing acknowledgment of off-grid living as a legitimate, sustainable lifestyle choice. This evolution of legal and societal attitudes toward off grid living marks a significant milestone in the movement's history, signaling a shift from the margins toward the mainstream of cultural consciousness.

In this historical reflection, the off-grid movement reveals itself as a living, breathing entity shaped by the currents of technological innovation, cultural shifts, and the timeless human quest for autonomy and harmony with the natural world. It stands as a mosaic of human endeavor, a tapestry woven from the threads of necessity, choice, tradition, and innovation. As we look to the future, this rich heritage offers not only inspiration but also valuable lessons in resilience, adaptability, and the enduring power of community. In the unfolding story of off-grid living, each individual and community who chooses this path contributes to the evolution of a movement that challenges, reimagines, and ultimately redefines what it means to live a good life in harmony with the earth.

EMBRACING TECHNOLOGY: TOOLS FOR MODERN OFF-GRID LIVING

In the tapestry of off-grid living, threads of innovation weave through the fabric of daily existence, binding the ancient wisdom of self-sufficiency with the modern marvels of technology. This fusion, far from diluting the essence of wilderness living, enhances its depth, broadening the horizon for those who seek independence from the grid while nurturing a harmonious relationship with the environment.

Digital Resources: A Gateway to Collective Wisdom

The digital age, with its vast repository of knowledge and community, offers a lifeline to the off-gridder. Online forums serve as bustling marketplaces of ideas where wisdom is traded and experiences are shared, from troubleshooting a temperamental solar setup to identifying edible wild plants. Here, the collective knowledge of countless individuals converges, providing answers, offering solace, and inspiring innovation. Apps, meticulously designed to cater to the specifics of off-grid living, transform smartphones into multifunctional tools. Whether it's mapping the sun's path to optimize solar panel placement or identifying constellations in the night sky, these digital companions become indispensable in the quest for self-reliance.

Renewable Energy Innovations: Harnessing Nature's Bounty

In the quest for energy autonomy, the sun, wind, and water emerge as faithful allies, their power captured through the ingenuity of human invention. Solar technology, with each advancement, pushes the boundaries of efficiency, turning even the most modest ray of sunlight into a source of power. Innovations in photovoltaic materials and designs promise a future where energy scarcity is a relic of the past. Wind turbines, too, have evolved, their blades slicing through the air with refined efficiency, capturing the breath of the earth to light homes and power machines. Hydropower, harnessed through micro-turbines in babbling brooks and mighty rivers, underscores the potential of perennial water flows as sources of ceaseless energy. Together, these technologies form the cornerstone of energy independence, transforming natural phenomena into reliable allies in the off-gridder's quest for autonomy.

Smart Systems: The Symphony of Efficiency

In the domain of off-grid living, efficiency is not merely a goal but a necessity. Smart systems, born from the marriage of technology and ingenuity, orchestrate the consumption and conservation of resources with precision. These systems monitor, control, and optimize the use of water, energy, and waste, ensuring that not a drop, not a watt, is squandered. Through sensors and automation, a greenhouse can regulate its temperature, a rainwater harvesting system can allocate water based on need, and a solar array can adjust its angle to capture the optimal amount of sunlight. This symphony of efficiency, conducted by smart systems, underscores the potential of technology to not only simplify but also significantly enhance the sustainability of off-grid living.

Technology as an Enabler: Simplifying the Complex

In the narrative of off-grid living, technology emerges not as a crutch but as a catalyst, an enabler of dreams once deemed too ambitious or complex. The daunting task of transitioning to a self-sufficient lifestyle is rendered manageable through tools and technologies that demystify the unknown. Drones map out the land, revealing the contours and characteristics that dictate the placement of homes and gardens. Water testing kits, compact and easy to use, ensure that the elixir of life flowing from streams and wells is safe for consumption. Even the humble smartphone becomes a gateway to knowledge, connecting the off-gridder to a world of information and innovation.

In this landscape, where technology intertwines with tradition, the off-gridder finds freedom. Freedom to harness the power of the wind without losing the touch of the earth; freedom to capture the warmth of the sun without casting a shadow on the land; freedom to draw water from the depths without muddying the waters of sustainability. Here, technology serves not to alienate but to connect, not to complicate but to simplify, weaving a life of independence with threads of innovation and strands of tradition.

In the embrace of technology, the modern off-gridder navigates the wilderness of independence with tools forged from the fires of human ingenuity. These tools, from the tangible to the intangible, from the mechanical to the digital, become extensions of the self, amplifiers of human capability. They remind us that in the quest for self-sufficiency, we are not alone but are supported by the collective wisdom of generations past and present, by the innovations of those who dared to dream of a life untethered, and by the endless possibilities that lie at the intersection of technology and the human spirit.

PLANNING YOUR OFF-GRID TRANSITION

❧

Amidst the canvas of life's vast possibilities, the decision to transition to an off-grid lifestyle stands as a declaration of independence, a move toward a life that values autonomy over convenience and sustainability over consumption. This decision, monumental in its implications, requires not just a leap of faith but a methodical approach grounded in clear vision, achievable goals, and an unwavering commitment to adaptability. It's akin to planting a garden; you start with a vision of lush abundance, plot out the beds with precision, and prepare for the unpredictable whims of weather, all the while nurturing the seedlings of your endeavor with patience and foresight.

SETTING ACHIEVABLE OFF-GRID GOALS

Vision and Objectives

Defining a clear vision for your off-grid transition is akin to sketching a blueprint before building a house. It involves a deep introspection about what you seek to achieve—be it independence, resilience against crises, a sustainable lifestyle, or a blend of all three. It's about painting a picture of your desired future with broad strokes and then refining it with the details that matter most to you. For example, envisioning a self-sufficient homestead powered by renewable energy, sustained by a permaculture garden, and designed with natural materials provides a guiding star for your endeavors.

Milestones

Establishing milestones translates your vision into actionable segments, making the monumental task of transitioning off-grid seem less daunting. Think of it as mapping out a long journey into checkpoints. Each milestone, whether it's securing a plot of land, completing a water harvesting system, or achieving a full season of food self-sufficiency, serves as a tangible marker of progress. It's important to celebrate these achievements, as they not only mark progress but also boost morale and motivation.

Flexibility

Flexibility is the undercurrent that sustains your transition, allowing you to navigate the unforeseen challenges that inevitably arise. This adaptability can be likened to a tree bending in the wind; it's about having a solid foundation rooted in your vision and objectives but being willing to adjust your plans as conditions change. Incorporating flexibility into your plans might mean having alternative solutions for water or power or being open to adjusting your timeline based on the availability of resources or changes in personal circumstances.

Success Criteria

Identifying what success looks like for your off-grid journey is crucial for maintaining direction and motivation. Success criteria can range from the tangible, such as achieving energy independence, to the intangible, like a sense of peace and connection with nature. It's about setting clear, measurable goals that reflect your values and vision and then regularly assessing your progress against these benchmarks. This ongoing evaluation ensures that you remain aligned with your objectives and allows for course corrections as needed.

Goal-Setting Worksheet

To aid in the planning of your off-grid transition, consider using a goal-setting worksheet that helps break down your vision into actionable objectives, milestones, flexible strategies, and success criteria. This worksheet can serve as a living document, evolving as your transition progresses.

1. **Vision Statement**: Write a detailed description of your ultimate off-grid lifestyle. What does it look and feel like?
2. **Objectives**: List the key objectives that will help you achieve this vision. Be specific and realistic.
3. **Milestones**: Break down each objective into tangible milestones. Assign a timeline to each milestone.
4. **Flexibility Plan**: For each objective, identify potential challenges and outline alternative strategies.
5. **Success Criteria**: Define what success looks like for each objective. How will you measure progress?

This structured approach to planning your off-grid transition not only clarifies the path ahead but also empowers you to navigate it with confidence and resilience. Remember, the goal is not to adhere rigidly to a predetermined plan but to remain committed to your vision while being adaptable to the twists and turns of the journey.

BUDGETING FOR YOUR OFF-GRID DREAM: A STEP-BY-STEP GUIDE

In the pursuit of an off-grid existence, financial acumen becomes as crucial as any survival skill, a beacon guiding you through the murk of unforeseen expenses toward the shores of self-sufficiency. The creation of a detailed budget stands as the first step in this financial voyage, a meticulous process that demands an honest assessment of both initial setup costs and the ongoing expenses that will weave through the fabric of off-grid living.

Financial Planning

Crafting a budget tailored to your off-grid aspirations begins with a granular breakdown of costs, delineating between the one-time expenses of establishing your homestead and the recurring costs that sustain it. Initial expenditures often encompass land acquisition, home construction or modification, and the installation of renewable energy systems. On the other hand, ongoing expenses might include maintenance of your systems, property taxes, and the cost of seeds for your garden. Diligence in this phase involves reaching out to professionals for quotes, researching the price of materials, and considering the cost of permits and legal fees. This thorough financial blueprint not only illuminates the path ahead but also fortifies you against the turbulence of unexpected costs.

Cost-Saving Strategies

The art of economizing without compromising the integrity of your off-grid setup emerges as a valuable skill in stretching your budget. One approach involves the strategic sourcing of materials, where salvage yards, online marketplaces, and community exchanges become treasure troves of affordable building supplies. Additionally, embracing the phased implementation of your project allows for the distribution of costs over time, easing the financial burden. For instance, prioritizing the establishment of your water harvesting system before expanding your solar array can optimize cash flow while ensuring progress. Moreover, investing time in acquiring new skills—be it carpentry, plumbing, or gardening—can substantially reduce labor costs, turning each DIY project into an opportunity for learning and growth.

Investment in Self-Sufficiency

Viewing each expense through the lens of investment transforms the financial landscape of off-grid living from a terrain of costs to a realm of value creation. This perspective recognizes that upfront expenditures in renewable energy systems, sustainable building materials, and land development are not mere purchases but investments in a lifestyle that promises autonomy, resilience, and harmony with the environment. For example, the initial outlay for a solar power setup, while significant, paves the way for energy independence, freeing you from the volatility of utility costs and contributing to your long-term financial stability. Similarly, investments in soil health and water conservation lay the groundwork for abundant gardens that nourish both body and soul, underscoring the interconnectedness of financial planning and sustainable living.

Tracking Expenses

Maintaining vigilance over your finances requires tools and methods that provide clarity and insight into your spending patterns. Spreadsheet software offers a versatile platform for tracking expenses, allowing for the categorization of costs, the tracking of actual spending against your budget, and the identification of areas where adjustments may be necessary. Additionally, budgeting apps designed for personal finance can streamline this process, offering features such as receipt scanning, expenditure analysis, and customizable alerts that keep you informed and engaged with your financial health. Regularly reviewing your financial status not only ensures adherence to your budget but also empowers you to make informed decisions, adapting your strategy in response to both challenges and opportunities.

In navigating the financial dimensions of off-grid living, you engage in a delicate dance with numbers, a dance that demands precision, foresight, and a willingness to adapt. This journey, marked by the meticulous planning of expenses, the strategic economization of resources, the insightful investment in self-sufficiency, and the diligent tracking of spending, unfolds as a testament to the depth of your commitment to a life unbound by the grid. Through this process, you lay the financial foundation upon which your off-grid dream is built, a foundation strong enough to support not just the physical structures of your homestead but the values and visions that inspired your journey.

NAVIGATING ZONING LAWS AND BUILDING CODES

In the intricate dance of transitioning to an off-grid lifestyle, an often-overlooked partner is the complex web of zoning laws and building codes that govern the physical space we aspire to transform. This network of regulations, while seemingly daunting, serves as the framework within which the safety and harmony of communities are maintained. For the aspiring off-gridder, a deep dive into the legalities surrounding their dream space is not just advisable but imperative. It's here, in the meticulous scrutiny of ordinances and statutes, that one often finds the line between aspiration and reality.

Legal Research

Embarking on legal research is akin to charting a course through a labyrinth, where each turn reveals new challenges and opportunities. The specificity of zoning laws and building codes to locales means that a strategy effective in one region may not hold water in another. This research extends beyond a mere Google search; it involves consultations with local planning departments, review of municipal and county ordinances, and, if necessary, engagement with legal professionals who specialize in land use. Understanding these regulations illuminates the boundaries within which one must operate, highlighting restrictions on land usage, building sizes, and the types of structures permitted. Armed with this knowledge, the off-grid transition plan can be tailored to align with legal requirements, ensuring that the dream of off-grid living does not falter on the rocks of regulatory non-compliance.

Permitting Process

Navigating the permitting process is a rite of passage for the off-grid enthusiast, a journey that demands patience, persistence, and meticulous attention to detail. This process typically begins with the submission of detailed plans that comply with local zoning and building codes, followed by a period of review by municipal authorities. Adjustments to plans may be required, necessitating a back-and-forth that can test the resolve of even the most determined. However, this interaction should not be viewed as adversarial but rather as an opportunity for collaboration. Local officials, often well-versed in the nuances of their regions' regulations, can provide invaluable guidance and suggestions for aligning one's off-grid aspirations with the legal framework. This phase, while potentially time-consuming, is crucial in laying the groundwork for a legally sound and sustainable off-grid existence.

Alternative Solutions

The path to off-grid living is not without its obstacles, particularly when conventional building methods and materials clash with local regulations. In these instances, the exploration of alternative solutions becomes a beacon of hope. Innovations in sustainable building, such as straw bale construction, earth ships, and cob houses, offer environmentally friendly alternatives that may also provide more flexibility in navigating zoning laws and building codes. However, the adoption of these methods often requires additional steps, including the education of local officials about their benefits and safety and, in some cases, the commissioning of studies or reports to demonstrate compliance with safety standards. This exploration of alternatives is not merely a means to circumvent restrictions but a genuine alignment of one's off-grid vision with sustainable practices and creative problem-solving.

Community Advocacy

The pursuit of off-grid living, for many, is emblematic of a deeper desire for a life that is in harmony with both nature and community. It is within this context that community advocacy emerges as a powerful tool for fostering understanding and effecting change. Engaging with local communities and authorities offers a dual opportunity: to educate others about the benefits and feasibility of off-grid living and to advocate for policies that are supportive of sustainable and self-sufficient lifestyles. This engagement can take many forms, from participating in town hall meetings and community forums to organizing workshops that showcase the practical aspects of off-grid living. The goal is to build bridges, fostering a dialogue that transcends mere compliance with existing regulations and moves toward the co-creation of policies that encourage and support sustainable development. Through this advocacy, the off-gridder becomes not just a solitary figure carving out a niche in the wilderness but an integral part of a community-wide movement toward resilience, sustainability, and mutual support.

In the grand scheme of transitioning to an off-grid lifestyle, the meticulous navigation of zoning laws and building codes, the patient wading through the permitting process, the creative exploration of alternative building solutions, and the proactive engagement in community advocacy are not mere bureaucratic hurdles. They are the threads that weave the fabric of a legally sound, community-supported, sustainable existence. This journey, marked by legal research, collaboration with authorities, innovation, and advocacy, is not a solitary endeavor but a communal dance, engaging with the very structures that govern our shared spaces. In embracing this process, the off-grid aspirant steps into a role that extends beyond personal ambition to encompass a wider commitment to the principles of sustainability, resilience, and community harmony.

SELECTING YOUR OFF-GRID LOCATION: CLIMATE AND LAND CONSIDERATIONS

Within the tapestry of decisions weaving the fabric of an off-grid life, the choice of locale stands paramount, a beacon guiding the way toward sustainable solitude or communal resilience. This choice, far from mere preference, is a complex calculus of environmental, logistical, and climatological factors, each bearing its unique weight on the scale of feasibility and fulfillment.

Geographical Analysis

Embarking on a geographical analysis of potential locales requires a meticulous evaluation of the land's character, its climate, topography, and the bounty—or scarcity—of natural resources it harbors. The terrain's contours, from the gentle slopes and inviting rainwater collection to the rugged hills, challenging but rewarding with wind power potential, dictate the methods and means of sustainable living tailored to each site. Proximity to natural water sources, the soil's fertility, and the availability of timber and stone not only influence the design and construction of an off-grid homestead but also its viability and impact on the surrounding ecosystem. This analysis, grounded in both research and reverence for the land, lays the groundwork for a harmonious existence with the natural world, ensuring that the chosen site offers not just shelter but sustenance and sustainability.

Accessibility

Accessibility, often overshadowed by the allure of seclusion, emerges as a critical consideration, influencing everything from daily logistics to emergency preparedness. The ideal locale strikes a delicate balance, offering refuge from the cacophony of modern life while remaining within reach of essential services and community connections. Access to roads, even those less traveled, ensures the flow of supplies, the feasibility of building projects, and the ability to welcome visitors or seek assistance when needed. Moreover, proximity to medical facilities, markets, and like-minded communities weaves a safety net, invisible but invaluable, providing peace of mind in the embrace of wilderness. This pragmatic approach to accessibility does not compromise the off-grid ethos but reinforces its foundation, ensuring resilience in the face of both the mundane and the unexpected.

Climate Resilience

In the shadow of climate change, resilience emerges as a guiding principle in the selection of an off-grid locale. A location's climate, with its patterns and extremes, shapes the strategies for building, energy generation, and food cultivation, demanding adaptability, and foresight. Regions prone to drought necessitate innovative water conservation and storage solutions, while areas frequented by storms or flooding call for robust, weather-resistant structures and contingency plans. This climate resilience, woven into the fabric of off-grid planning, ensures that the chosen locale not only supports a sustainable lifestyle but also withstands the capricious moods of nature. It is in this alignment with the climate's rhythms and challenges that an off-grid homestead finds its strength, turning potential vulnerabilities into testimonies of human ingenuity and resilience.

Environmental Impact

At the heart of off-grid living lies a profound respect for the environment, a commitment to tread lightly on the earth that sustains us. Evaluating the potential environmental impact of an off-grid setup on the surrounding area transcends mere compliance with regulations; it is an ethical imperative, a reflection of the values that propel individuals toward this lifestyle. This evaluation encompasses the conservation of natural habitats, the protection of water quality, and the minimization of soil disturbance, ensuring that the land's integrity and biodiversity are preserved. Renewable energy systems, sustainable waste management practices, and eco-friendly building materials are not just choices but commitments to this ethos, reflecting a deep understanding of the interconnectedness of all life. In selecting a location for off-grid living, this commitment to minimizing environmental impact guides decisions, shaping a lifestyle that seeks not only independence from societal grids but also harmony with the natural world.

In the intricate dance of selecting a location for off-grid living, where every step is measured against the rhythms of nature and the realities of human needs, the fabric of an off-grid dream is woven. This process, grounded in geographical analysis, accessibility considerations, climate resilience, and a commitment to minimizing environmental impact, is both a challenge and a privilege. It demands not just a keen eye for the practicalities of off-grid living but also a heart attuned to the subtle languages of the land and climate. Through this meticulous approach to selecting a locale, the foundation for a sustainable, resilient, and harmonious off-grid existence is laid, setting the stage for the realization of a dream that is as old as humanity itself: to live in balance with the natural world, free from the constraints of conventional grids but deeply connected to the earth and its rhythms.

DESIGNING AN OFF-GRID HOME: PRINCIPLES AND PRACTICES

In the pursuit of crafting a dwelling that epitomizes the ethos of off-grid living, the confluence of design principles rooted in energy efficiency, sustainable material use, functional spatial organization, and a profound integration with nature becomes paramount. This endeavor, far from a mere architectural exercise, is an intimate dialogue with the environment, a deliberate act of shaping a habitat that not only shelters but also sustains, enriches, and minimizes its imprint on the natural world.

Energy-Efficient Design

At the core of an off grid home's blueprint, the imperative for energy efficiency demands a meticulous orchestration of design elements to optimize natural heating, cooling, and lighting, thereby reducing reliance on mechanical systems. The strategic orientation of the home to capture the sun's trajectory, especially in colder climates, becomes a linchpin in this design philosophy. Large, south-facing windows invite winter sunlight to penetrate living spaces, warming them naturally, while overhangs or deciduous trees screen the high summer sun, keeping interiors cool. Further, the incorporation of thermal mass materials like stone or concrete in floors or walls serves to absorb and store heat during the day, releasing it slowly as temperatures drop, a natural alchemy that maintains comfort without the constant draw on energy resources. Ventilation, too, plays a critical role, with the design facilitating cross breezes that cool the home naturally, reducing or eliminating the need for air conditioning. This symbiosis between design and nature, leveraging the earth's rhythms, lays the foundation for a home that stands as a testament to self-sufficiency.

Sustainable Materials

The selection of materials in the construction of an off-grid home transcends aesthetic considerations, embedding within it a commitment to sustainability and environmental stewardship. The emphasis on locally sourced, sustainably harvested, or recycled materials minimizes the environmental cost of transportation and production, linking the home's physical structure to the local ecosystem in a tangible expression of respect and reciprocity. Bamboo, with its rapid regrowth rate, offers a renewable resource for flooring and cabinetry, while reclaimed wood tells a story of reclamation and renewal, bringing a sense of history and character to the home. Adobe and rammed earth materials with deep historical roots offer not only sustainability credentials but also exceptional thermal performance, their mass acting as a natural regulator of interior temperatures. In the conscious choice of these materials, the off-grid home becomes a physical embodiment of the principles of sustainability, each element a reflection of a broader ethos of care for the planet.

Functional Layout

The internal organization of an off-grid home and its spatial layout adhere to the principle of functionality, ensuring that each square foot serves a purpose that reflects the lifestyle and values of its inhabitants. This approach to design prizes multipurpose spaces that adapt to varying needs, transforming from work areas to dining spaces or guest accommodations with fluid ease. Storage solutions become creative and integrated, utilizing vertical spaces, hidden compartments, and built-in furniture to minimize clutter and maximize livability. The kitchen, often the heart of the home, is designed for efficiency and sustainability, with space for food preservation techniques like canning and drying, reflecting the off-gridder's connection to their food sources. This thoughtful approach to layout ensures that the home not only accommodates the practical aspects of off-grid living but also nurtures the social and emotional well-being of its occupants, creating spaces that foster connection, creativity, and rest.

Integration with Nature

Perhaps the most profound principle guiding the design of an off-grid home is its integration with the surrounding environment, a seamless blending of the built and natural worlds that diminishes boundaries and fosters a deep connection with the land. This integration manifests in design choices that extend the living space outdoors through decks, patios, or large doors that erase the line between inside and out. It is visible in the selection of a site that minimizes disruption to the natural landscape, preserving mature trees, natural watercourses, and wildlife habitats. Landscaping with native plants not only reduces water use but also supports local ecosystems, inviting birds, pollinators, and other wildlife to become part of the living tableau of the home. Green roofs and living walls take this integration vertical, offering not only insulation and air purification benefits but also a visceral reminder of the home's symbiosis with nature. In these ways, the off-grid home does not merely sit on the land but converses with it, a dialogue of form, function, and philosophy that honors the intrinsic value of the natural world.

In this meticulous crafting of an off-grid home, where energy efficiency, sustainable materials, functional design, and integration with nature converge, the resulting structure stands as much more than a place of residence. It becomes a manifesto of off-grid living, a physical articulation of values that champion self-sufficiency, sustainability, and a profound respect for the natural world. This home, forged from the earth and inspired by the sky, becomes a sanctuary, a place where the boundaries between human aspiration and natural grace blur, offering a model for living that is both ancient and urgently contemporary.

COMMUNITY BUILDING: FINDING LIKE-MINDED NEIGHBORS

In the realm of off-grid living, the fabric of community weaves a tapestry rich with the hues of shared endeavor, mutual support, and the collective wisdom of diverse experiences. This network, transcending the mere geographical, fosters a kinship rooted in common aspirations, challenges, and triumphs. The art of community building, therefore, becomes a pivotal element in the larger mosaic of off-grid life, offering a wellspring of resources, inspiration, and camaraderie.

Networking

The lattice of connections that form the backbone of any thriving community requires deliberate effort to initiate and nurture. Strategies for weaving these links vary, with digital platforms offering a global reach to find those whose paths parallel your own. Social media groups, forums dedicated to sustainable living, and websites catering to the off-grid community serve as conduits for these connections, allowing for the exchange of ideas, solutions, and stories. In parallel, the physical world offers equally fertile ground for connections. Local workshops, conferences on sustainability, and groups focused on skills like permaculture or renewable energy are not just learning opportunities but arenas for serendipitous meetings that can seed lasting relationships. Through these channels, the solitary endeavor of forging an off-grid life opens into a landscape peopled with allies, mentors, and friends.

Community Projects

Collaboration on projects that benefit the wider community or environment acts as a crucible for deepening these nascent ties. Joint ventures, whether establishing a community garden, building a shared renewable energy system, or organizing a local clean-up, not only accomplish tangible goals but also cultivate a sense of shared purpose and mutual reliance. Such projects become a dance of cooperation, where each participant's skills and knowledge contribute to a harmony greater than the sum of its parts. In this shared space of endeavor, relationships are fortified, skills are honed, and the vision of a sustainable, interconnected community finds expression in the physical world.

Mutual Support

The scaffold of mutual support that underpins any resilient community offers both a safety net and a springboard for its members. Systems of exchange, whether formal, like tool libraries or seed banks, or informal, like rotating help on individual projects, ensure that resources are maximized, and assistance is at hand when needed. This reciprocity extends to knowledge sharing, with experienced members mentoring newcomers and everyone contributing their unique expertise. In times of crisis, this network becomes vital, offering practical aid and emotional support, ensuring that no one faces challenges in isolation. Through this interdependence, the community not only survives but thrives, its members buoyed by the strength of their collective resources and resilience.

Cultural Exchange

At the heart of any community lies the rich soil of cultural exchange, where diverse backgrounds, experiences, and perspectives cross-pollinate, yielding new insights, innovations, and understandings. This exchange, respectful and open, enriches the community, broadening its collective worldview and enhancing its adaptability. Celebrations, shared meals, storytelling nights, and skill-sharing sessions become venues for this cultural dialogue, fostering an environment of learning and mutual respect. In this atmosphere, differences are not just tolerated but valued as sources of strength and growth, contributing to the vibrant tapestry of the off-grid community.

In the cultivation of community among like-minded neighbors, the off-grid life transcends the individual, blossoming into a collective endeavor that enriches all involved. Through networking, collaboration on community projects, systems of mutual support, and the ongoing exchange of cultures and ideas, this community becomes a living entity, pulsating with the energy of shared purpose and the warmth of kinship. It stands as a testament to the power of connection, not just to the land but to one another, forming a web of relationships that supports, inspires, and propels its members toward their shared vision of a sustainable, resilient life.

As this chapter draws to a close, we are reminded of the integral role community plays in the off-grid journey. From the initial threads of connection woven through networking to the collaborative endeavors that strengthen these bonds, the value of finding and nurturing relationships with like-minded individuals cannot be overstated. Mutual support and cultural exchange further enrich this experience, creating a vibrant, dynamic community that is both a source of practical aid and a wellspring of inspiration. This communal aspect of off-grid living not only enhances the individual experience but also contributes to the larger movement toward sustainability and self-sufficiency, demonstrating the profound impact of collective action and shared values. As we move forward, the importance of community remains a guiding light, illuminating the path to a life that is not only off the grid but deeply connected to the human spirit and the natural world.

WATER AND FOOD SELF-SUFFICIENCY: THE FOUNDATION OF OFF-GRID LIVING

❦

Water, in its ceaseless flow, carves the contours of the land, nourishing life in its myriad forms. It is both a symbol and a source of life, an element so essential that our very existence hinges upon it. In the world of off-grid living, where the umbilical cord to municipal supplies is severed, mastering the collection, storage, and purification of rainwater becomes not just a skill but a sacred duty. It is here, in the dance of droplets cascading from the heavens, that we find the rhythm of resilience, a harmony with nature that sustains and enriches our lives beyond measure.

RAINWATER HARVESTING SYSTEMS: SETUP AND MAINTENANCE

System Design

Selecting the right rainwater harvesting system involves careful consideration of climate, landscape, and the needs of your homestead. It's akin to tailoring a suit: precision matters. In regions with sporadic, heavy downpours, a system with ample storage capacity and rapid collection capability is key. Conversely, areas with frequent, light rains might benefit from a setup that maximizes surface area for collection. The design starts with calculating your water needs, factoring in drinking, cooking, bathing, and gardening requirements. From there, the roof becomes your catchment area, its material and slope influencing the quality and quantity of water collected. Gutters, downspouts, and first-flush diverters then guide the water to storage tanks, which should be sized based on your calculated needs, with a buffer for dry spells.

Installation Tips

When installing gutters and storage tanks, attention to detail can make or break your system. Gutters should have a slight slope toward downspouts, ensuring efficient water flow and minimizing stagnation. Positioning tanks at a higher elevation, if the landscape allows, uses gravity to feed water into your home, reducing the need for pumps. When placing tanks, consider accessibility for maintenance and proximity to areas of use to minimize water loss in distribution. Secure tanks on a solid foundation to prevent shifting and check local regulations for any restrictions or requirements regarding rainwater collection systems.

Maintenance Routines

Regular maintenance ensures your system runs smoothly and safely. Monthly inspections of gutters, downspouts, and screens keep the pathways for water clear of debris. Cleaning your storage tanks annually prevents sediment buildup and bacterial growth. Testing water quality periodically, especially if used for drinking, should be part of your routine. A simple visual check for clarity, smell, and taste can alert you to potential issues, with more comprehensive testing available through local extension services or environmental agencies.

Legal Considerations

Understanding the regulations around rainwater collection in your area is crucial. While many regions encourage rainwater harvesting, others have restrictions or require permits. This legal landscape can dictate the design and capacity of your system. A call to your local planning department or a consultation with an environmental lawyer can provide clarity, ensuring your system complies with state and local laws and avoiding any legal headaches down the road.

Rainwater Harvesting Checklist

To streamline the planning and maintenance of your rainwater harvesting system, consider the following checklist:

Design Phase:

- Calculate water needs based on household size and garden requirements.
- Assess roof material and slope for optimal catchment.
- Choose storage tanks with sufficient capacity and space for your needs.
- Plan gutter and downspout placement for efficient water collection.

Installation Phase:

- Install gutters with a slight slope toward downspouts.
- Position storage tanks on a solid foundation, preferably at an elevation.
- Install first-flush diverters to improve water quality.

Maintenance Phase:

- Inspect gutters and downspouts monthly and clear any debris.
- Clean storage tanks annually to prevent sediment buildup.
- Test water quality periodically, especially for drinking purposes.

Legal Phase:

- Check local regulations and obtain any necessary permits.
- Ensure your system design complies with state and local laws.

This checklist not only serves as a roadmap for setting up and maintaining your rainwater harvesting system but also as a reminder of the ongoing commitment required to sustain this vital component of off-grid living. Through diligent planning, installation, and maintenance, coupled with an understanding of legal requirements, your rainwater harvesting system can provide a reliable, sustainable water source, anchoring your homestead in the principles of self-sufficiency and environmental stewardship.

WATER PURIFICATION TECHNIQUES FOR WILDERNESS SURVIVAL

In the wilderness, where the veneer of civilization thins and nature presents itself in its rawest form, the quest for potable water becomes a primal need. This need transcends mere survival. Within this context, the mastery of water purification techniques emerges as a vital skill, a bridge between the abundant yet often untamed waters of the natural world and the sanctuary of a self-sufficient existence.

Boiling and Distillation

The transformation of water through heat, from a liquid to a vapor and back to a liquid, is a dance as ancient as time. Boiling, the simplest form of purification, leverages this transformation to eliminate pathogens. The process requires a heat source, a vessel, and patience as water must maintain a rolling boil for at least one minute, though at higher altitudes, three minutes is prudent due to the decrease in boiling temperature. The purity achieved through boiling is unparalleled, yet the method demands significant fuel and time, making it less feasible for large quantities of water.

Distillation, a sophisticated cousin of boiling, involves capturing steam and condensing it back into liquid, a process that not only eradicates biological contaminants but also separates water from dissolved solids and chemicals. The apparatus for distillation can be as rudimentary as a pot with a concave lid or as complex as a purpose-built distiller, but all operate on the same principle. While distillation's ability to render even the most compromised water potable is remarkable, its requirement for substantial energy input and the cumbersome nature of distillation equipment often relegates it to a method of last resort.

Chemical Treatment

The alchemy of water purification finds another expression in the use of chemicals, specifically iodine and chlorine, agents that, in small doses, are safe for humans yet lethal to microorganisms. Iodine, favored for its efficacy against a broad spectrum of pathogens, imparts minimal taste alteration, making it suitable for short-term use, especially in colder environments where its effectiveness is not diminished. Conversely, chlorine, available in various forms from liquid to tablets, offers a robust solution for purifying large volumes of water, its potency undeterred by temperature. However, the residual taste and the potential health risks associated with prolonged use prompt caution, making these chemicals allies best summoned with discretion.

Filtration Systems

In the sieve through which nature's impurities are sifted, filtration systems stand as sentinels guarding against the unseen threats that lurk in unprocessed water. Portable filters, compact and designed for individual use, operate either by pump action or gravity, drawing water through media that trap pathogens while allowing clean water to pass. Their efficacy varies with the pore size of the filter media, with smaller pores offering greater protection at the cost of flow rate. Stationary systems, intended for base camps or homesteads, scale this concept, providing a higher volume of purified water through more complex assemblies that might include multiple stages of filtration and even ultraviolet light treatment for additional safety. While filtration systems offer a balance between convenience and effectiveness, their reliance on mechanical parts and the need for regular maintenance and replacement of filter elements temper their utility with a measure of responsibility.

Natural Purification

In the embrace of the wilderness, the methods of water purification extend beyond the mechanical to the embrace of natural processes. Solar water disinfection (SODIS), a method as simple as it is elegant, utilizes the sun's ultraviolet light to neutralize pathogens in clear plastic bottles exposed to sunlight for six to forty-eight hours, depending on the intensity of the sun. This method, while dependent on climatic conditions, requires no resources beyond sunlight and time, making it an invaluable technique in the off-grid arsenal.

Sand filters, another ally borrowed from nature, mimic the earth's own filtration system, using layers of sand and gravel to remove particulates and pathogens from water. The construction of a sand filter can range from a simple container filled with sand to more elaborate setups with graded layers of sand and gravel, each designed to catch smaller particles as water moves through the system. Though slow and requiring regular maintenance to clean or replace the sand, these filters offer a sustainable option for those committed to living in harmony with the land.

In the wilderness, where every drop of water tells a story of the earth's abundance and fragility, the knowledge and application of these purification techniques become a testament to the human spirit's adaptability and respect for nature. From the primal simplicity of boiling to the sophisticated alchemy of distillation, the calculated efficacy of chemical treatment, the balanced functionality of filtration systems, and the elegant simplicity of natural purification methods, each technique offers a path to securing one of life's most precious resources. In this quest, the off-gridder becomes both student and steward, learning from the land and giving back through the careful, respectful use of its bounty, ensuring that the water that sustains also remains pure and plentiful for generations to come.

STARTING AN ORGANIC GARDEN: FROM PLANNING TO HARVEST

Garden Planning

In the realm of self-sufficiency, the organic garden stands as a testament to the enduring connection between land and sustenance, a space where cycles of life unfold with the passing seasons. The initial act of sketching the garden's layout demands more than a mere allocation of space; it requires an intimate dialogue with the land, an understanding of its contours, and an acknowledgment of the sun's daily passage overhead. This understanding guides the placement of beds, ensuring that leafy greens find solace in the shade while sun-loving tomatoes bask in the light. The choice of crops, far from arbitrary, aligns with the rhythms of the local climate, the length of growing seasons, and the intricacies of frost dates. This harmony between crop selection and environmental conditions minimizes struggle and maximizes yield, turning the garden into a reflection of the land's inherent bounty.

Soil Preparation

The soil, a living tapestry teeming with microorganisms, acts as the foundation upon which the garden thrives. Preparing this soil, then, is not merely an act of turning and tilling but a rite of enrichment, a way of giving back to the earth that sustains us. The introduction of organic matter, whether through the incorporation of compost, the layering of mulch, or the application of natural fertilizers, invigorates the soil. Compost, the alchemy of kitchen scraps and garden waste transformed into nutrient-rich humus, feeds the soil and, by extension, the plants that call it home. Mulching, a practice as practical as it is ancient, conserves moisture, suppresses weeds, and adds organic matter back to the soil as it decomposes. Natural fertilizers, from the simplicity of manure to the complexity of fish emulsion, provide targeted nutrients, supporting the garden's diverse needs. This thoughtful preparation of the soil, a blend of science and intuition, sets the stage for a garden that is not just productive but vibrant with life.

Pest Management

In the dance of growth and decay, pests emerge not as mere nuisances but as participants in the garden's ecological ballet, their presence both a challenge and an opportunity. Organic strategies for pest management eschew the harshness of chemical interventions, opting instead for approaches that enhance the garden's natural defenses and preserve its ecological balance. Companion planting, an age-old practice, leverages the synergistic relationships between certain plants to deter pests, attract beneficial insects, and improve crop health. The strategic introduction of predator species, whether ladybugs to combat aphids or birds to manage caterpillars, acts as a natural check on pest populations. Barriers and traps, from the simplicity of netting to protect against birds to the ingenuity of pheromone traps for specific insects, provide physical solutions to pest challenges. This approach to pest management, grounded in observation and adaptation, respects the garden's place within the broader ecosystem, turning potential adversaries into allies in the quest for balance and bounty.

Harvesting Tips

The act of harvesting, far from a mere conclusion to the growing season, is a nuanced practice that honors the garden's yield and anticipates future growth. Timing is critical, with each vegetable and fruit possessing its moment of peak ripeness, a window where flavor and nutritional content converge. Techniques vary, from the gentle twist that frees a tomato from its vine to the careful cut that harvests leafy greens while encouraging new growth. The handling of produce, too, demands care, ensuring that fruits and vegetables arrive from the garden to the table with their vitality intact. Post-harvest, the garden itself requires attention, with the removal of spent plants and the addition of compost setting the stage for the next cycle of growth. This rhythm of harvesting, a blend of art and science, encapsulates the garden's role in the off-grid life, a source of sustenance, a center of learning, and a place of connection to the cycles of nature.

In every seed planted, in every bed nurtured, and in every harvest celebrated, the organic garden emerges as a microcosm of the off-grid ethos, a space where self-sufficiency and sustainability find expression in the soil and the soul. This garden, born from careful planning, enriched soil, balanced ecosystems, and thoughtful harvesting, stands as a testament to the resilience and bounty of the living earth, a reminder of the simple truth that in giving back to the land, we receive gifts far greater than the sum of our labors.

FORAGING FOR WILD EDIBLES: SAFETY AND SUSTAINABILITY

In the dappled light of the forest floor, nature spreads a feast of wild edibles, an array of flavors unknown to the conventional palate. This bounty, freely offered by the land, requires not the toil of the plow but the wisdom of the forager, a knowledge steeped in the lore of the land and the cycles of the seasons. To forage is to engage in an ancient dialogue with nature, one that nourishes the body and the spirit, connecting us to the earth in the most primal way. Yet, this communion demands respect, a keen awareness of the delicate balance that sustains these ecosystems, and the acumen to partake without harm.

Identifying Edible Plants

The skill to distinguish between the nourishing and the noxious in the wild is foundational for the forager. This discernment relies not on guesswork but on a detailed study of plant characteristics, from the vein patterns on leaves to the texture of stems and the shape of flowers. Field guides, both digital and printed, become invaluable tools in this education, offering visual cues and descriptive texts that guide the forager's hand. Workshops led by seasoned foragers and botanists further enrich this learning, providing hands-on experiences that embed this knowledge deeply. Yet, caution remains paramount, for nature's mimicry can deceive, leading the unwary to mistake the poisonous for the palatable. Thus, the rule of thumb for foragers is clear: When in doubt, leave it out.

Ethical Foraging

To forage with ethics is to walk gently on the earth, taking only what is needed and leaving no trace of one's passage. This principle ensures that the wild spaces that provide these edibles remain vibrant and bountiful for generations to come. Ethical foraging dictates a restraint, where only a fraction of what is available is harvested, allowing populations to regenerate and thrive. It respects the roles these plants play in their ecosystems, as food for wildlife or as part of the habitat's structural integrity. Areas under environmental protection or private lands are honored as off-limits, preserving these spaces from human intrusion. In practicing these guidelines, foragers act not as conquerors but as stewards, their harvest a gift from the earth, received with gratitude and care.

Preparation and Preservation

The transformation of wild edibles from raw ingredients into culinary delights or preserved treasures is an art, one that honors the unique flavors and nutritional profiles of these plants. Simplicity often guides preparation, allowing the intrinsic qualities of the edibles to shine, whether sautéed greens revealing a hint of bitterness or berries bursting with untamed sweetness. Preservation, too, follows the rhythms of nature, with drying, fermentation, and canning extending the bounty of the seasons into the leaner months. Drying herbs and mushrooms preserve their essence, while fermentation unlocks new flavors and augments nutritional value. Canning, though requiring meticulous attention to safety, offers a way to savor the taste of wild fruits and vegetables long after their season has passed. Through these methods, the forager turns the ephemeral gifts of the earth into enduring nourishment, bridging the gap between the abundance of the present and the needs of the future.

Avoiding Hazards

The forager's path, while rich with rewards, is fraught with hazards, from the venomous bite of plants masquerading as benign to the invisible threat of contamination. Knowledge becomes the shield against these dangers, with the study of toxic plants as critical as the identification of edible ones. This education delineates the harmful substances these plants harbor, from the liver-damaging toxins of certain mushrooms to the cyanide precursors in wild almonds. Contamination, too, poses a significant risk, with industrial pollutants, agricultural runoff, and even naturally occurring compounds like arsenic tainting potential harvests. Foragers must thus be judicious in their choice of foraging sites, avoiding areas near roads, industrial sites, or treated agricultural fields. Testing soil and water, when possible, offers further assurance of safety, ensuring that the purity of the wild edibles matches their wild origins. In navigating these hazards with caution and knowledge, foragers ensure that their communion with the earth remains safe, sustainable, and enriching.

In the embrace of the wild, where nature lays out a feast of untamed flavors and ancient nourishment, foraging stands as a testament to human connectivity with the land. It is a practice that demands respect, knowledge, and a profound sense of responsibility, ensuring that the act of taking is always balanced with the act of giving back. Through careful identification, ethical harvest, thoughtful preparation, and vigilant avoidance of hazards, foraging becomes not just a means of sustenance but a profound expression of living in harmony with the natural world, a dance of give and take that nourishes both the body and the soul.

INTRODUCTION TO AQUAPONICS: COMBINING FISH AND PLANTS

In the realm of sustainable agriculture, aquaponics emerges as a symphony of aquatic life and vegetation, a system where the waste produced by farmed fish supplies nutrients for plants grown hydroponically, which in turn purify the water. This closed-loop system, an epitome of efficiency and harmony, stands as a beacon for off-gridders and environmental stewards alike, illuminating a path toward food security and ecological balance.

The essence of aquaponics lies in its fusion of aquaculture and hydroponics, a marriage that mitigates the drawbacks of each while amplifying their benefits. Here, the excretions from fish transform, through bacterial action, into a rich source of nitrogen, feeding a diverse array of plants suspended in water without soil. This cycle not only creates a self-sustaining food production system but also significantly reduces water usage compared to traditional farming methods. Moreover, the absence of soil negates the need for chemical fertilizers, heralding a new era of organic cultivation.

Embarking on the construction of an aquaponics system requires meticulous planning but rewards with abundance. Initial considerations involve selecting a location that balances sunlight exposure for plants with the temperature needs of fish, often necessitating partial shading or greenhouse cover in warmer climates. The choice between a media-based, nutrient film, or deep-water culture system influences this decision, each offering distinct advantages in terms of complexity, cost, and scalability.

The foundation of a basic aquaponics setup begins with the assembly of two primary components: a fish tank and a grow bed. The fish tank, typically made from durable, non-toxic materials, houses the aquatic life, its size dictating the system's overall capacity. Above it, the grow bed, filled with a lightweight, inert medium like expanded clay pellets or gravel, supports the plants. A water pump circulates nutrient-rich water from the fish tank to the grow bed, where plants absorb the nutrients before the cleansed water returns to the fish, completing the cycle. An air pump, essential for oxygenating the water, ensures the health of both fish and the beneficial bacteria crucial for nutrient conversion.

Selecting compatible plants and fish for the system is an art, balancing growth rates, temperature preferences, and nutritional needs. Leafy greens such as lettuce, kale, and herbs thrive in aquaponic environments, and their rapid growth rates make them ideal candidates. Simultaneously, fruit plants, though more nutrient-demanding, add diversity to the harvest, with tomatoes, peppers, and cucumbers as popular choices. In the aquatic domain, species like tilapia, catfish, and carp adapt well to aquaponic life, their hardiness and growth rates complementing the system's dynamics. Yet, the choice of fish extends beyond these practical considerations, reflecting personal preferences, culinary tastes, and local regulations on aquaculture.

Maintaining the health and productivity of an aquaponics system hinges on regular monitoring and intervention. Water quality tests, focusing on pH, ammonia, nitrite, and nitrate levels, guide the adjustment of feeding rates and water changes, preventing toxic accumulations, and ensuring the system's balance. Plant inspections include noting signs of nutrient deficiencies or pest infestations and prompt corrective actions, from adjusting the nutrient flow to introducing organic pest control measures. Similarly, observing fish for signs of stress or disease enables early interventions, safeguarding the aquatic population's vitality.

Troubleshooting an aquaponics system often involves detective work, tracing symptoms back to their causes. Unusual plant growth or discoloration might signal nutrient imbalances, necessitating a review of fish health, feeding practices, or the biofilters efficiency. Fish lethargy or loss, on the other hand, could indicate water quality issues, prompting a reassessment of aeration, filtration, or the system's stocking density. Through this process, challenges become opportunities for learning, each adjustment bringing the system closer to its ideal state of harmony and productivity.

In the broader narrative of off-grid and sustainable living, aquaponics stands as a testament to human ingenuity and the potential for coexistence with the natural world. It offers a model of agriculture that transcends the limitations of traditional farming, promising a future where food production aligns with ecological principles, conserving water and land while providing nutritious, chemical-free produce and protein. This system, a microcosm of efficiency and balance, encapsulates the ethos of off-grid living, where independence is achieved not in isolation but through a deep, symbiotic relationship with the environment. In embracing aquaponics, we affirm our commitment to a life that is sustainable, resilient, and in harmony with the earth, a life where each cycle of growth and renewal brings us closer to the ideals of self-sufficiency and ecological stewardship.

PRESERVING YOUR HARVEST: CANNING, DRYING, AND FERMENTING

In the rhythm of off-grid life, where the bounty of the earth meets the ingenuity of human efforts, preserving the harvest becomes a testament to foresight and self-reliance. The acts of canning, drying, and fermenting are not merely methods of preservation but rituals that bind us to the cycles of abundance and scarcity, allowing us to store the essence of one season for the nourishment of the next. Through these practices, we not only secure our food supply but also engage in a dialogue with tradition, learning the age-old arts of extending the life of our harvest.

Canning Essentials

Canning invites us into a world where the flavors of the garden are sealed within glass, a process that marries heat with acidity to create an environment hostile to spoilage organisms. The division between water bath canning for high-acid foods like fruits and tomatoes and pressure canning for low-acid items such as vegetables and meats delineates the boundaries of safety within which we operate. Sterilization of jars and lids forms the bedrock of this practice, a nonnegotiable step that ensures the purity of the environment where our food will be stored. The meticulous attention to processing times and temperatures, dictated by the nature of the food and the altitude of the canning site, ensures that each jar is both a time capsule of flavor and a bulwark against foodborne illness. Through canning, we not only preserve the bounty of our gardens and foraging expeditions but also weave a thread of continuity between the past and the future, our pantries becoming libraries of taste and nutrition.

Drying Techniques

Drying, the oldest form of food preservation, harnesses the elements to draw moisture from our harvest, leaving behind concentrated flavors and extended shelf life. The sun, a benevolent ally in this process, offers its rays as a gentle means of dehydration, requiring only time and airflow to transform slices of fruit or herbs into shriveled jewels of nutrition. Ovens, with their controlled heat, accelerate this process, allowing for the drying of a wide array of produce, from tomatoes to apples, each item requiring vigilant monitoring to ensure optimal dryness without scorching. Dehydrators, specialized in their function, circulate warm, dry air through trays of food, achieving consistent results with minimal effort. This methodical removal of water not only concentrates flavors and nutrients but also creates a bulwark against decay, extending the usability of our harvest far beyond its natural lifespan.

Basics of Fermenting

Fermentation, a magical alchemy facilitated by microorganisms, transforms the simple into the sublime, the perishable into the preserved. This ancient practice, found in cultures around the globe, relies on the metabolic processes of bacteria or yeast to convert sugars into acids, gases, or alcohol, imbuing foods with complex flavors, improved digestibility, and enhanced nutritional profiles. Vegetables submerged in brine become crunchy, tangy pickles, their colors and flavors deepened by the fermentative process. Dairy, inoculated with specific cultures, thickens into yogurts and cheeses, each variety a testament to the transformative power of microbes. Beverages, from the effervescence of kombucha to the creamy tang of kefir, offer probiotic benefits alongside their refreshing taste. In embracing fermentation, we not only preserve our harvest but also engage in a partnership with the invisible world of microorganisms, a collaboration that enriches our diet and connects us to the web of life.

Storage and Safety

The culmination of our preservation efforts lies in the careful storage of our canned, dried, and fermented goods, a task that demands both organization and vigilance. Cool, dark, and dry spaces shield these treasures from the degradation of light, heat, and moisture, ensuring that the flavors and nutrients locked within remain intact. Regular inspection of stored items for signs of spoilage, from the bulging of can lids to the presence of mold on fermented foods, acts as a safeguard against the consumption of compromised goods. Through this attentive stewardship of our preserved harvest, we not only ensure the safety and quality of our food but also honor the effort and resources invested in its production.

In the act of preserving our harvest, we engage in a timeless dance with nature, a dance that spans the seasons and links us to generations past and future. Through canning, drying, and fermenting, we capture the fleeting abundance of the present, transforming it into a resource that sustains us through the leaner times. This cycle of abundance, preservation, and nourishment embodies the essence of off-grid living, where self-reliance and sustainability form the bedrock of our existence. As we close this chapter on preserving our harvest, we carry with us the knowledge and skills to secure our food supply, a fundamental pillar of our journey toward a life in harmony with the natural world.

SHELTER AND ENERGY INDEPENDENCE

❧

In the quest for off-grid living, the creation of shelter stands as a testament to human resilience and ingenuity, a tangible manifestation of the desire to live harmoniously within the confines of nature's bounds. This chapter delves into the heart of establishing a sanctuary that not only provides protection from the elements but also embodies the principles of sustainability and self-reliance. The convergence of choosing materials, integrating design principles, applying construction techniques, and adhering to permitting and codes form the pillars upon which durable and energy-efficient habitats are built.

DESIGNING AND BUILDING YOUR OFF-GRID SHELTER

Choosing Materials

The selection of materials for constructing an off-grid shelter requires more than a nod to aesthetic appeal; it demands a commitment to durability and sustainability. Materials like reclaimed wood not only tell a story of resilience but also reduce the environmental footprint by repurposing resources that would otherwise end up in landfills. Meanwhile, bamboo emerges as a champion of eco-friendly construction, with its rapid growth rate and tensile strength making it a renewable powerhouse. The use of locally sourced stone and earth not only minimizes transportation emissions but also blends the structure into the landscape, paying homage to the local environment.

Design Principles

Incorporating passive solar design into the blueprint of an off-grid home ensures that the sun's bounty is harnessed to its full potential, providing natural heating and lighting. This principle involves orienting the structure to maximize southern exposure, allowing windows to flood living spaces with warmth and light during the winter months while overhangs shield interiors from the scorching summer sun. The incorporation of natural insulation, such as straw bales or cellulose, further envelops the home in a cocoon of efficiency, maintaining comfortable temperatures year-round without reliance on external energy sources.

Construction Techniques

Exploring construction techniques unveils a spectrum of possibilities, from the time-honored traditions of timber framing and cob building to modern innovations like structural insulated panels (SIPs). Timber framing, an art as old as civilization itself, offers a blend of beauty and strength, its interlocking timbers providing structural integrity without the need for nails or screws. Cob building, with its mixture of clay, sand, straw, and water, invites hands-on participation, transforming construction into a communal activity that connects builders with the earth. SIPs, prefabricated panels that sandwich insulation between two structural facings, promise efficiency and speed, and their modular nature reduces construction time and thermal bridging.

Permitting and Codes

Navigating the maze of permits and codes is less of a hurdle and more of a dialogue with the stewards of land use and safety regulations. This dialogue begins with a thorough understanding of local zoning laws and building codes, illuminating the path to compliance, and ensuring that the envisioned shelter meets all legal requirements. It's akin to mapping a river before setting sail; understanding its currents and eddies ensures a smoother journey. Engaging with building officials early and often, armed with detailed plans and a spirit of cooperation, transforms this process into a collaborative effort that secures the foundation of the off-grid home within the framework of communal standards.

Off-Grid Shelter Planning Checklist

To aid in the planning and execution of your off-grid shelter, consider the following checklist:

Materials Selection:

- Inventory available reclaimed materials and local resources.
- Evaluate the sustainability and durability of potential materials.
- Consider the environmental impact and energy efficiency of each option.

Design Principles:

- Determine the optimal orientation for passive solar gain.
- Plan window placement for natural lighting and seasonal temperature regulation.
- Incorporate natural insulation options into the design.

Construction Techniques:

- Research traditional and modern construction methods suitable for your climate and terrain.
- Consider the availability of local labor and community participation.
- Plan for the use of prefabricated elements to reduce construction time.

Permitting and Codes:

- Review local zoning laws and building codes relevant to off-grid structures.
- Schedule consultations with building officials to discuss your plans.
- Prepare detailed drawings and documentation for permit applications.

This checklist serves as a compass, guiding the planning stages of your off-grid shelter project, ensuring that every decision aligns with the principles of sustainability, efficiency, and legal compliance. Through meticulous planning, informed material selection, thoughtful design, and adherence to construction standards, the creation of an off-grid shelter transcends mere habitation, becoming a sanctuary that reflects the ethos of off-grid living.

SOLAR POWER SETUP: FROM PANELS TO BATTERIES

In the realm of off-grid living, the adoption of solar power emerges not merely as a choice but as a declaration of independence from traditional energy sources, a step toward self-reliance and harmony with the environment. Navigating the intricacies of a solar power setup unveils a landscape where technology meets the primal force of the sun, transforming it into a conduit for sustainable living. This section unfolds the layers involved in understanding system components, guiding you through the installation process, and outlines the essentials of maintenance and monitoring, culminating in an analysis of cost considerations.

System Components

The anatomy of a solar power system reveals a network of components, each playing a pivotal role in the conversion of sunlight into usable electricity. At the heart lie the solar panels "stalwart workers" that capture the sun's energy. The selection of panels involves a balance between efficiency, cost, and the physical constraints of the installation site. Following the panels, the charge controller stands as a guardian, regulating the flow of electricity to the batteries, preventing overcharging, and enhancing their lifespan. Batteries, the reservoirs of energy, store electricity for use when sunlight is scarce. Their capacity and type dictate the system's ability to meet energy demands. An inverter completes the circuit, translating the direct current (DC) stored in batteries into the alternating current (AC) used by household appliances. Understanding these components and their interplay is crucial for anyone venturing into the world of solar power, providing a foundation upon which a resilient and efficient system can be built.

Installation Process

The installation of solar panels unfolds in a sequence of carefully calibrated steps, beginning with the assessment of the site. Optimal placement ensures maximum exposure to sunlight, with considerations for angle, orientation, and the avoidance of shade. Mounting the panels, whether on rooftops or ground-based structures, demands precision and adherence to safety standards, ensuring they remain secure against the elements. Wiring connects the panels to the charge controller, introducing a pathway for the flow of electricity, while batteries, strategically positioned, become the repository for this energy. The final connection to the inverter bridges the system to the home's electrical network, completing the circuit that brings solar power from the abstract to the tangible. Throughout this process, adherence to local codes and regulations ensures compliance and safety, turning the vision of solar-powered living into reality.

Maintenance and Monitoring

Sustaining the efficiency of a solar power system necessitates a regimen of maintenance and monitoring, a commitment to the vigilance that preserves its longevity and performance. Routine inspections of panels for dirt, debris, or damage enhance their efficiency, ensuring the unobstructed conversion of sunlight. Charge controllers and batteries, too, require scrutiny, with connections checked for corrosion and wear and battery levels monitored to avoid deep discharges. The inverter, as the system's electrical heart, demands regular testing to confirm its operational integrity. Beyond physical maintenance, monitoring systems, from simple voltage meters to sophisticated software, offer real-time insights into energy production and consumption, allowing for adjustments that optimize performance. This proactive approach to maintenance and monitoring not only extends the life of the system but also maximizes the return on investment, ensuring solar power remains a pillar of off-grid sustainability.

Cost Analysis

The financial landscape of solar power, with its initial outlay and long-term savings, presents an equation where the benefits extend beyond mere economics, touching on values of environmental stewardship and energy independence. The cost of components, installation, and permits forms the bulk of upfront expenses, a figure mitigated by potential subsidies, incentives, and the decreasing cost of solar technology. When juxtaposed with the ongoing costs associated with traditional energy sources, the investment in solar power reveals its true value over time. Savings on utility bills, coupled with the low maintenance costs of solar systems, translate into a return on investment that extends beyond dollars and cents, embodying the priceless benefits of resilience, sustainability, and harmony with the natural world. Calculating this return involves not just the assessment of financial savings but also the valuation of environmental and personal values, painting a comprehensive picture of the true cost and reward of solar power in off-grid living.

In this exploration of solar power setup, from the intricacies of system components and the precision of the installation process to the diligence of maintenance and the calculus of cost analysis, the narrative unfolds as a journey toward autonomy and sustainability. It is a testament to the power of harnessing the sun's energy, a step toward a future where off-grid living is not just feasible but flourishing, powered by the clean, endless energy provided by our closest star.

WIND TURBINES FOR THE HOMESTEADER: A DIY GUIDE

In the pursuit of energy autonomy, wind turbines stand as stellar workers capturing the ceaseless dance of air currents to generate power. This section unfolds the fabric of understanding wind energy's role in off-grid living, guiding you through the process of constructing a wind turbine, identifying the prime location for its installation, and weaving it into the tapestry of a holistic energy system.

The essence of wind power lies in its simplicity and elegance—a turbine's blades catch the wind, initiating a ballet of rotation that drives a generator to produce electricity. The beauty of this system lies not only in its operation but in its potential to transform the mercurial nature of wind into a reliable source of energy. For those seeking refuge from the grid's confines, wind energy offers a path to electrical independence, its viability cemented by advancements in technology that afford efficiency and durability. The allure of harnessing this resource rests on its ubiquity and the promise of reducing one's ecological footprint, making it an appealing choice for the eco-conscious homesteader.

The adventure of constructing a wind turbine from scratch or assembling one from a kit invites a hands-on experience that demystifies the technology, turning abstract concepts into tangible reality. For the DIY enthusiast, kits provide a streamlined avenue, offering pre-engineered components that ensure compatibility and ease of assembly. These kits serve as a bridge, offering a guided experience that instills confidence through structured guidance and support. Conversely, building a turbine from scratch caters to those craving a deeper connection with their energy system, allowing for customization that tailors the turbine to specific needs and site conditions. This route, though more challenging, rewards with a profound sense of accomplishment and a unique insight into the mechanics of wind power generation.

Choosing the optimal location for a wind turbine transcends mere convenience, delving into an analysis of wind patterns, topography, and obstacles that might impede airflow. The quest for the perfect site mirrors the search for a wellspring, where factors such as elevation and clearance from surrounding obstructions converge to dictate the turbine's efficiency. An elevated position, free from the turbulence created by buildings, trees, and terrain, enables the turbine to access steadier, stronger winds, maximizing energy production. This careful siting, informed by an understanding of the land and its wind profile, ensures that the turbine operates within the sweet spot of its capacity, turning the invisible force of the wind into a palpable stream of electricity.

Integrating wind power with solar and other energy sources weaves a resilient energy system, a tapestry rich with diversity that guards against the intermittent inherent in renewable resources. This hybrid approach, embodying a philosophy of redundancy and balance, ensures a steady supply of power, adapting to the shifting moods of nature. Solar panels, basking in the sun's glow, complement the turbine's efforts, their combined forces creating a synergy that smooths the ebbs and flows of energy availability. The incorporation of battery storage acts as a reservoir, capturing excess energy for use during calm or cloudy periods, ensuring a seamless flow of power to the homestead. This integrated system, a microcosm of harmony and innovation, stands as a testament to the possibilities that unfold when diverse energy sources unite under the banner of sustainability.

In this exploration of wind turbines for the homesteader, from the foundational understanding of wind energy to the hands-on experience of turbine construction, the selection of an optimal site, and the strategic integration with other energy sources, the narrative unfolds as an invitation to embrace the wind's untapped potential. It's an invitation to step into a realm where the air itself fuels our independence, offering a lifeline to those seeking to carve out a sustainable existence free from the constraints of traditional power grids.

THERMAL MASS HEATERS: EFFICIENT OFF-GRID HEATING

Within the fabric of off-grid living, the quest for warmth during the cold embrace of winter leads to innovations rooted in ancient wisdom yet refined by modern understanding. Among these, thermal mass heaters emerge as stalwarts, their principle of operation a testament to the harmonious interplay between fire, stone, and air. These heating systems, distinguished by their ability to store vast quantities of heat and release it slowly over time, offer a paradigm shift in the approach to off-grid heating, marrying efficiency with the primal comfort of radiant warmth.

The underlying mechanism of thermal mass heaters revolves around the concept of heat storage within dense materials. As fire dances within the heater's core, the surrounding masonry—a meticulously arranged labyrinth of firebrick, soapstone, or cob—absorbs the heat, becoming a reservoir of warmth. Unlike conventional wood stoves that expel most of their heat directly into the air, often resulting in rapid temperature fluctuations, thermal mass heaters bask in a slow burn, releasing their stored warmth gradually. This process ensures a consistent temperature over extended periods, minimizing fuel consumption while maximizing comfort.

Embarking on the construction of a thermal mass heater demands a detailed blueprint that considers the specific needs and layout of the home. The foundation of this endeavor lies in choosing the right materials, those capable of withstanding high temperatures while possessing excellent heat retention properties. Firebrick forms the core, and its refractory nature can endure the intense heat of combustion. Surrounding this, materials like soapstone or cob serve as thermal mass, and their density is key to the system's efficiency. The design intricately weaves together these materials, creating a path for smoke and heat that maximizes exposure to the thermal mass before exiting through the chimney. This pathway, often serpentine in nature, ensures that by the time smoke leaves the system, its heat has been thoroughly transferred to the surrounding masonry.

Fuel efficiency stands at the heart of the thermal mass heater's appeal, a beacon for those seeking to reduce their ecological footprint while living off-grid. The secret to this efficiency lies not only in the design and materials but also in the method of combustion. By employing a top-down burn, where fire consumes from the top layer of wood downward, the heater achieves a complete combustion of fuel, reducing emissions and ash while extracting every ounce of available heat. This method, coupled with the slow release of warmth from the thermal mass, means that a single firing can warm a home for a day or more, depending on the outside temperature and the insulation of the dwelling.

Safety, an ever-present concern when fire is involved, permeates every aspect of a thermal mass heater's construction and use. Adherence to building codes and standards ensures that the heater not only performs optimally but also poses no threat to the home or its inhabitants. This adherence extends to the placement of the heater, ensuring it is located away from combustible materials, and to the construction of the chimney, which must provide adequate draft while preventing backdrafts. Regular inspections and maintenance of the system, particularly the chimney and firebox, further mitigate risks, ensuring that the heater remains a source of comfort and not a concern.

In the realm of off-grid heating, thermal mass heaters stand as monuments to the synergy between human ingenuity and the elemental forces of fire and stone. Their operation, a ballet of heat absorption and release, offers a model of efficiency and sustainability that resonates with the ethos of off-grid living. The construction of these heaters, a blend of science and art, demands precision and understanding but rewards with a system that warms not only the body but also the soul, a constant reminder of the simplicity and beauty inherent in living close to the land.

NATURAL COOLING TECHNIQUES FOR OFF-GRID HOMES

In realms where the off-grid ethos intertwines with the relentless ascent of temperatures, the quest for refuge from the heat necessitates not just solutions but a reimagining of habitation itself. This reimagining beckons forth a symbiosis of architectural ingenuity and the inherent cooling beneficence offered by nature, crafting abodes that breathe with the land, eschewing mechanical dependencies for a delicate balance of shade, airflow, and the earth's own tempering pulse.

Passive Cooling Strategies

The architecture of air, invisible yet palpable in its influence, becomes a sculptor of comfort within the off-grid home. Openings positioned to capture prevailing breezes transform into conduits for natural ventilation, orchestrating a flow that exhales warmth and inhales coolness. This design, mindful of window placements and door alignments, invites cross-ventilation, leveraging differences in air pressure to animate a home with the breath of the earth. Further, the strategic incorporation of thermal chimneys acts as a siren call to warm air, enticing it upward and out, allowing cooler air to settle in its stead. Such strategies, devoid of mechanical intervention, align the home with the rhythms of the natural world, ensuring a habitat that remains resilient in the face of rising mercury.

Shading and Insulation

The sun, at its zenith, casts a brilliance that, though life-giving, can turn the interior of a home into a crucible. Here, the art of shading reclaims comfort, casting a veil over the harshness of direct sunlight. Overhangs, those protruding eyebrows of a home, shield windows from the high summer sun while permitting the lower winter sun to warm the interiors. Pergolas, clothed in verdant vines, create living patios that breathe coolness into adjacent spaces. Similarly, the role of insulation transcends its wintertime connotation, becoming a barrier against heat penetration. Materials with high thermal resistance encase the home, reflecting heat away and maintaining the sanctuary within as a reprieve from the external blaze. This dual strategy of shading and insulation stands as a bulwark against heat, ensuring that the home remains a refuge regardless of the sun's intensity.

Evaporative Cooling

Water, in its evaporation, steals warmth from the air, a phenomenon that becomes a cooling grace within the off-grid home. The use of water features, from the simplicity of a birdbath to the complexity of a courtyard fountain, introduces this cooling effect into the domestic landscape, subtly lowering temperatures with each cycle of evaporation. For areas where dry air prevails, evaporative coolers offer a more pronounced application of this principle, drawing warm air through water-saturated pads and releasing it as a cooler breeze. This method, though contingent on climate, harnesses a fundamental physical process to imbue the home with coolness, marrying efficiency with the elemental beauty of water.

Landscaping for Cooling

The land itself, when whispered to in the language of thoughtful landscaping, responds with shade, moisture, and cooled breezes. Trees, those stalwart allies positioned to shield the home from the sun's arc, not only offer shade but also transpire, releasing moisture into the air that further cools the surroundings. The choice of vegetation, favoring native species accustomed to the local climate, ensures a landscape resilient in the face of heat, requiring minimal intervention to thrive. Ground covers, in their spread, protect the soil from the sun, keeping it cool and adding to the overall cooling effect. This living architecture, a collaboration between plant life and human dwelling, creates microclimates of coolness, enveloping the home in an embrace that shields it from the heat. Through this interplay of flora and structure, the off-grid home becomes not just an isolated entity but a part of a cooler, breathable landscape. Its comfort is woven from the very fabric of its surroundings.

In navigating the warmth that seasons bring to bear, these natural cooling techniques unfold as chapters in a larger narrative of sustainable living. They speak of an alignment with the environment, where homes breathe with the land, shaded, and insulated by thoughtful design, cooled by the evaporation of water, and nestled within landscapes that temper the air. This approach, rooted in passive strategies and the inherent properties of materials and plant life, charts a course toward habitats that stand in defiance of heat, not through conquest but through harmony, ensuring that the off-grid home remains a bastion of comfort in the warmth of the sun's embrace.

DIY INSULATION STRATEGIES TO MAXIMIZE ENERGY EFFICIENCY

Within the quiet sanctum of an off-grid dwelling, the battle against the elements—be it the piercing cold of winter or the oppressive heat of summer—rests heavily on the shoulders of insulation. This silent guardian, often hidden within the walls, underfoot, or overhead, serves as the first line of defense in maintaining the internal climate, a buffer between the comfort of the interior and the whims of the external environment. The choice between natural and synthetic insulation materials is not merely a matter of economics or availability but a profound decision that reflects a commitment to environmental stewardship and personal health.

Natural insulators, derived from renewable resources, offer a breath of purity in an often synthetic-laden world. Sheep's wool, with its crimped fibers creating pockets of air, provides exceptional thermal and acoustic insulation while managing humidity with natural ease. Cellulose, recycled paper treated for fire resistance, stands as a testament to the potential of repurposed materials, its loose-fill form adaptable to irregular spaces, and offering superior air-sealing capabilities. Hemp insulation, another contender, brings not only thermal efficiency but also carbon sequestration into the home, its fibers locking away carbon for the lifetime of the building. Each of these materials, in their essence, carries the narrative of the earth, a narrative of renewal and resilience.

Conversely, synthetic insulators, born from human ingenuity, present a spectrum of performance and versatility. Polystyrene, in its expanded form, offers a lightweight solution with high resistance to moisture, making it ideal for below-grade applications. Polyurethane foam, sprayed into crevices and cavities, expands to create an unbroken thermal barrier. Its effectiveness is measured in its ability to curtail air movement and moisture intrusion. These synthetic options, while effective, carry the weight of their production processes and end-of-life disposal, considerations that must be balanced against their insulative properties.

The act of insulating a home goes beyond material selection, delving into the craftsmanship of installation. Walls, the vertical canvases of our living spaces, demand precision in the placement of insulation, ensuring no gaps or compression compromise its effectiveness. Roofs, our shelters from the sky, benefit from an ample layer of insulation, a cap that retains warmth in winter and deflects heat in summer. Floors, in contact with the earth or air beneath, act as conduits for temperature exchange, where insulation serves to dampen this dialogue, maintaining the desired climate within. Each of these applications, executed with meticulous care, transforms raw materials into a cohesive system that stands vigilant against energy loss.

Windows, the eyes of the home, offer a view of the world but also represent a critical point of thermal exchange. The installation of energy-efficient windows, with multiple panes and inert gas fills, creates a barrier to heat transfer, an invisible shield that maintains the integrity of the home's thermal envelope. Complementing these advanced windows, thermal curtains offer a layer of fabric insulation, a simple yet effective means of augmenting window performance. Drawn against the night or the high sun, these curtains act as thermal blankets, preserving the energy within.

Air sealing, the final frontier in the quest for energy efficiency, targets the invisible leaks that undermine the home's thermal integrity. Doorways, windows, and points of ingress for utilities become focal points for this endeavor. Caulking and weatherstripping, applied with a careful hand, fill these breaches, crafting an airtight seal that holds the interior climate constant. This meticulous process of identification and sealing not only enhances comfort but also reduces the demands on heating and cooling systems, a direct contribution to the home's energy efficiency.

In this nuanced exploration of insulation materials, installation techniques, window solutions, and air sealing, one finds not just strategies for energy efficiency but a deeper narrative of balance and harmony. The materials chosen, natural or synthetic, reflect a commitment to the environment and personal well-being. The craftsmanship in installation, a dedication to excellence and efficiency. The enhancement of windows and the diligence of air sealing are a testament to the meticulous care invested in creating a sanctuary that stands resilient against the elements. This narrative, woven from the threads of material science, construction techniques, and environmental philosophy, underscores the foundational role of insulation in the tapestry of off-grid living, a role that ensures the home not only shelters but also sustains.

As we close this exploration, the synthesis of materials, methods, and mindful strategies presents a blueprint for off-grid dwellings that embody efficiency, sustainability, and resilience. This approach, rooted in a deep understanding of insulation's pivotal role, lays the groundwork for homes that harmonize with their environment, offering comfort and security in the embrace of nature.

SHARE THE GIFT OF SELF-SUFFICIENCY

"I've lived a slower and less expensive life going off the grid, and I'm happier because of it."

— ED BEGLEY JR

Off-grid living may have been considered an "alternative" lifestyle in past decades, but today, close to 1.7 billion people embrace this lifestyle to a certain extent and in the U.S., around 250,000 feel it is right for them.

A myriad of world events have sparked the off-grid movement, with 2020 in particular being a stark reminder of how quickly things can shift and how important nature is to our health and well-being. For many, simply being outside, embracing an active lifestyle, and benefiting from the stress-busting effects of nature are enough to merit greater prioritization of the Great Outdoors in their day-to-day lives. Of course, going off-grid celebrates nature in a much more powerful way, enabling human beings to lower their carbon footprints dramatically.

Throughout this book, I have aimed to show you that once you decide to go off-grid, making it happen is a matter of following a list of steps, all of which I have provided in detail. Thus far, we have seen how essential budgeting, knowing local zoning laws and building codes, and selecting the right location are. You have also learned vital skills such as how to choose an energy-efficient design, create a like-minded community, and find the water and food you need to thrive off-grid.

If this book has inspired you to start taking steps to live in a freer, more independent way, then I hope you can share your thoughts with others.

By leaving a short review of this book on Amazon, you'll show other readers who are interested in sustainable living where they can find the information they need to take them from newbies to confident, self-sufficient off-gridders.

Thank you for your support. Together, we can create a supportive community that shares information, resources, and experience.

Scan the QR code below:

HEALTH, SAFETY, AND
EMERGENCY PREPAREDNESS

In the embrace of the wilderness, where the grid fades into the rearview mirror, and the land stretches out, raw and untamed, the air carries a different weight—a reminder of our intrinsic vulnerability and the necessity of preparedness. Here, the knowledge of first aid becomes more than just a skill; it morphs into a lifeline, a beacon of hope in moments where seconds count and help is miles away. This chapter unfurls the tapestry of emergency medical skills, from the immediate response to the tender art of wound care, the vital rhythms of CPR, and the ancient wisdom of natural remedies. It's in these pages that the language of survival speaks, teaching hands to heal, minds to stay calm, and spirits to persevere.

FIRST AID SKILLS FOR WILDERNESS EMERGENCIES

Immediate Response

Imagine the snap of a branch underfoot, a misstep, and then a tumble—a common enough scenario in the rugged embrace of nature. In that moment, the ability to assess the situation swiftly and respond with clarity can pivot the outcome from tragedy to relief. The cornerstone of immediate response lies in the ABCs—Airway, Breathing, and Circulation—ensuring that vital functions are supported. Assessing consciousness, clearing obstructions from the airway, and monitoring breathing and circulation form the bedrock of the first response, setting the stage for further care or evacuation if necessary.

Wound Care

In the wilderness, even minor wounds demand attention, their potential to escalate into serious infections heightened by the remote setting. The process begins with cleaning, using water—boiled and cooled or disinfected with iodine tablets—to flush out debris. Dressing the wound follows with sterile dressings or, in their absence, the cleanest cloth available. Bandages then secure the dressing, applying pressure to stem the bleeding and protect the wound from further contamination. This meticulous care mirrors the layers of the earth itself—a cleansing rain, a protective layer of soil, and the pressure that forms mountains, each step vital to healing.

CPR and Emergency Procedures

There's a rhythm to life, often taken for granted until it falters. Cardiopulmonary resuscitation (CPR), a symphony of chest compressions and breaths, seeks to sustain that rhythm when the heart and lungs pause. The technique demands precision—

compressions at a depth of two inches for adults, at a rate of 100 to 120 per minute, interspersed with breaths that inflate the lungs without overfilling them. For children, the approach adjusts, and the balance of force and frequency is fine-tuned to their smaller frames. This life-saving dance, performed with hope and urgency, becomes a bridge across the chasm of cardiac arrest, holding space for survival against the odds.

Natural Remedies

The wilderness, for all its perils, also holds a pharmacy in its flora, offering remedies honed through generations of traditional knowledge. For inflammation, the willow, with its salicin-rich bark, offers a natural precursor to aspirin. Aloe vera, it's cool gel tucked within spiny leaves, soothes burns with gentle efficiency. For cuts, plantain leaves, often dismissed as weeds, can be crushed, and applied to staunch bleeding and reduce infection risk. These natural allies, woven into the fabric of first aid, remind us of the deep connection to the land, a bond that heals and nurtures even in the face of adversity.

Wilderness First Aid Checklist

Immediate Response:

- Check ABCs: Airway, Breathing, Circulation.
- Assess consciousness and look for signs of shock.
- Clear airway if obstructed and monitor breathing.

Wound Care:

- Clean the wound with disinfected water.
- Dress in sterile dressing or the cleanest cloth available.
- Secure with a bandage and apply pressure if necessary.

CPR and Emergency Procedures:

- Chest compressions: 100 to 120 per minute, with a depth of two inches for adults.
- Breaths: Ensure not to overinflate lungs.
- Adjust technique for children as needed.

Natural Remedies:

- Willow bark for inflammation.
- Aloe vera for burns.
- Crushed plantain leaves for cuts.

This checklist serves as a beacon, guiding you through the fog of emergency with steps that ground, heal, and save. It's a testament to the power of preparedness, a declaration that even in the wilderness, far from the touchstones of civilization, resilience and recovery find a way.

CREATING A COMPREHENSIVE OFF-GRID MEDICAL KIT

In the remote embrace of a life untethered from the grid's pulsing current, the preparation of a medical kit transcends the mere accumulation of supplies; it becomes a curated collection of hope, a tangible manifestation of foresight, and a bastion against the unforeseen. This kit, a guardian of well-being, must be tailored, dynamic, and reflective of the unique challenges posed by the environment and the individual needs of its keeper.

Essential Supplies

At the heart of this assemblage lie the instruments and materials poised to address a spectrum of ailments and injuries, a repertoire of items selected not for their quantity but for their quality and versatility. Sterile gauze, adhesive bandages of various sizes, antiseptic wipes, and antibiotic ointment form the first line of defense against the intrusion of infection into wounds. Tools such as tweezers for the removal of foreign objects, scissors for cutting dressings, and a digital thermometer for monitoring fevers become extensions of one's intent to heal. Medications, both over the counter and prescription, require careful consideration; anti-inflammatory drugs, antihistamines for allergic reactions, and pain relievers stand ready to alleviate discomfort and prevent conditions from escalating. Rehydration salts, vital in the battle against dehydration, a likely adversary in the wilderness, underscore the importance of maintaining fluid balance in the body's quest for recovery.

Customization for Needs

The act of customizing this kit is akin to weaving a tapestry, where each thread represents an aspect of the user's health profile, environmental challenges, and personal risks. For those with chronic conditions, such as asthma or diabetes, the inclusion of specific medications and monitoring devices is not optional but essential. The climate, too, dictates its terms; in regions where venomous creatures dwell, antivenom becomes a critical component, while cold climates necessitate the addition of hypothermia treatments. This process of customization does not end with the assembly of the kit but evolves, a reflection of changing health needs, seasons, and acquired skills, ensuring that the kit remains a living document of preparedness.

Maintenance and Storage

The integrity of this collection, however, hinges not only on its initial assembly but on a regimen of maintenance that guards against the degradation of its components. Periodic reviews, scheduled with the change of seasons or following any use, serve to assess each item's condition, expiration dates, and quantities, ensuring that the kit remains in a state of perpetual readiness. The choice of storage container is waterproof and durable, protects against moisture and pests, and preserves the efficacy of the contents. A designated space, accessible yet protected from the elements, ensures that the kit remains a beacon of safety and that its location and contents are known to all members of the household or group.

Training and Knowledge

Yet, for all its carefully chosen contents, the true power of the medical kit lies not within its fabric confines but in the knowledge and training of those who wield it. Basic first aid training, a foundation upon which more advanced skills can be built, empowers individuals to use the kit's contents with confidence and precision. This education, whether acquired through formal classes, online courses, or community workshops, illuminates the path from panic to action, transforming fear into a focused response. The inclusion of manuals or guides within the kit itself acts as a silent tutor, offering reminders and guidance in moments of uncertainty. For those who venture into the wilderness, where the mantle of caretaker may fall upon their shoulders, this training becomes not just an asset but a necessity, a layer of preparedness that complements the physical components of the kit.

In the creation of a comprehensive off-grid medical kit, the journey from selection to assembly, customization, maintenance, and education is a testament to the resilience and resourcefulness of those who choose to step away from the grid's embrace. This kit, a microcosm of preparedness, stands as a sentinel against adversity, a tool not of fear but of empowerment, ensuring that health and safety remain within reach, even in the heart of the wilderness.

FIRE SAFETY AND MANAGEMENT IN THE WILDERNESS

In the sanctuary of the wilderness, where nature's tranquility and wild temperament converge, the act of igniting a fire carries with it an age-old aura of survival and comfort. Yet, within this act lies a dual responsibility: to harness its warmth and guard against its voracious appetite for destruction. The cultivation of safe fire practices becomes not merely a skill but a sacred duty, ensuring that the flames that cook our meals and ward off the night's chill do not turn into the harbingers of catastrophe.

Safe Fire Practices

The foundation of preventing wildfires in an off grid setting rests on a bedrock of respect for and understanding of the environment. It begins with the selection of a site for the fire, a clear, barren patch of earth embraced by stones, far removed from the whispering dry grass and the watchful trees. This precaution, coupled with the diligent clearing of debris and the establishment of a perimeter free from flammable materials, sets the stage for control. The size of the fire, kept modest and manageable, reflects a mindfulness that tempers the desire for warmth with the imperative of safety. A cache of water, or a shovel nearby, stands ready, prepared to quell any errant sparks that seek to escape the confines of their birthplace.

Fire Creation and Management

The ignition of a fire, an act as primal as it is essential, demands precision and care. Employing a method that layers tinder, kindling, and fuel allows the fire to breathe and grow, nurtured by the careful tending of its keeper. The maintenance of this living entity, with its heart of embers and its cloak of flames, involves a constant vigil, ensuring that it neither starves for lack of fuel nor rages out of control. As the shadows lengthen and the time comes to bid the fire farewell, the method of extinguishment becomes a ritual of respect for the force that has provided warmth and light. Dousing with water, stirring the ashes, and feeling for any remnants of heat ensure that the fire, once a companion through the hours of darkness, leaves no trace of its existence save for the memories of its warmth.

Protecting Your Homestead

The off-grid home, a haven within the untamed wilderness, requires protection from the indiscriminate fury of wildfires. This shield takes form in the creation of defensible space, a buffer that starves an approaching fire of fuel. The meticulous management of vegetation, the pruning of trees, and the removal of dead limbs and leaves diminish the chances of the home becoming fuel for an encroaching blaze. The choice of materials in the construction of the homestead itself reflects an awareness of fire's nature; non-combustible siding, fire-resistant roofing, and the installation of ember-resistant vents and eaves create a fortress against the flames. These measures, woven into the fabric of the homestead's existence, stand as a testament to the foresight and commitment to coexist with the wilderness while mitigating the threats it may pose.

Emergency Evacuation Plan

In the dance of flames and smoke, when the wind carries the scent of an approaching wildfire, the value of an emergency evacuation plan becomes immeasurable. This plan, crafted with clarity and practiced with diligence, maps the path from danger to safety. It delineates routes of escape, clear and unobstructed, leading away from the threat and toward refuge. The assembly of an evacuation kit, portable and packed with essentials—documents, medications, supplies—ensures readiness when the moment to leave arrives. Communication, the thread that binds a group or family together in times of crisis, relies on predetermined channels and rendezvous points, ensuring that even when separated by circumstance, reunification remains a beacon of hope. The practice of this plan, a rehearsal of calm amidst the storm of panic, ingrains its steps into the muscle memory of its participants, transforming uncertainty into action when the sky darkens with smoke.

In this realm where humans tread lightly on the earth, seeking not dominion but harmony, the management of fire—a force as old as time itself—becomes a reflection of this ethos. It underscores a relationship with the land that is based not on conquest but on stewardship, a pact sealed with the understanding that the flames that warm and feed also hold the power to destroy. Through the meticulous practice of safe fire creation and management, the fortification of the homestead against the ravages of wildfire, and the preparation for evacuation, this balance is maintained, ensuring that the wilderness remains a sanctuary, not just for the off-gridder but for all the life that calls it home.

EMERGENCY SIGNALING TECHNIQUES FOR RESCUES

In the vast expanse of wilderness, where solitude wraps around you like a dense fog, the ability to signal for help morphs into a critical lifeline, slicing through the silence and distance to touch the outer world. This art of communication, crafted from desperation and ingenuity, becomes a beacon for those lost or in peril, guiding rescuers through the labyrinth of nature to the source of the call.

Visual Signals

The landscape itself offers a canvas for visual signals, messages etched against the earth or sky, visible from afar. Mirrors, with their reflective sheen, capture the kiss of sunlight, transforming it into a gleaming signal capable of reaching the eyes of search teams or passing aircraft. The technique demands not just the possession of a signaling mirror but an understanding of how to angle it, catching the sun's rays and directing them purposefully, creating flashes that pierce the visual monotony of the wilderness. Smoke, another ally, speaks in billows and plumes, rising above the tree line to declare one's location. The creation of a smoke signal requires a fire, its size, and materials meticulously chosen to produce the dense, white smoke that contrasts starkly against the green and blue of nature. Adding green foliage or rubber to a fire increases the smoke's thickness, transforming a simple campfire into a beacon for rescue.

Sound Signals

When visibility is constricted, as it often does in the dense embrace of the woods or the veil of night, sound signals cut through the silence, carrying messages of distress across distances. Whistles, compact yet powerful, serve as the voice of the stranded, their sharp, piercing sound distinct from the natural chorus of the wilderness. The cadence of whistle blasts—three in succession—has become an internationally recognized distress signal, a call that transcends language barriers. Banging objects, whether metal against rock or sticks against trees, creates an auditory marker, a patterned noise that draws attention to its unnatural rhythm amidst the forest's symphony. These sound signals, reliant on repetition and pattern, become threads that searchers can follow, weaving through the auditory landscape to find their source.

Creating Markers

Markers, physical manifestations of one's presence, stand as silent sentinels pointing the way to rescue. Constructing these requires an eye for visibility and an understanding of symbols that convey distress. Triangles, an arrangement of three logs or stones, communicate universal signals of emergency, their geometric clarity a stark contrast to the organic chaos of nature. Similarly, arrows, constructed from branches or etched into the soil, guide rescuers in the direction of the stranded, each one a breadcrumb on the path to salvation. The positioning of these markers, in open clearings or along well-traveled paths, maximizes their chances of discovery, each one a testament to the hope and determination of those awaiting rescue.

GPS and Tech for Emergencies

In this era, where technology intertwines with even the most remote corners of existence, GPS devices and satellite messengers emerge as heralds of safety, their signals a bridge between the lost and the world beyond. GPS devices, once the purview of military and scientific communities, now offer civilians the power to pinpoint their location with startling accuracy, transforming a bewildering maze of wilderness into a mapped grid of longitude and latitude. Satellite messengers, compact and rugged, allow for communication beyond the reach of cell towers, sending distress signals and location data at the push of a button. The preparation for journeys into the unknown thus includes not just the packing of gear but the charging of these devices, the registration of their signals with rescue services, and the understanding of how to deploy them when all other paths to safety have vanished.

In the crucible of survival, where every second stretches with the weight of eternity, these techniques and tools stand as beacons of hope. They are the threads that bind the individual to the collective, the lost to the found. They serve not just as methods of signaling for rescue but as symbols of the human will to persevere, to reach out across the void and find a hand waiting in the darkness.

NATURAL DISASTER PREPAREDNESS: STAYING SAFE OFF-GRID

Identifying Risks

Inherent to the fabric of the earth are the caprices of nature— floods that swell rivers beyond their banks, hurricanes that lash the coastlines with ferocity, and earthquakes that tremble the ground underfoot. Each locale whispers its own tales of potential calamity, a language of risk inscribed in the landscape. Grasping these whispers necessitates a keen observation of historical patterns and geological markers, a study that unveils the threats particular to one's chosen sanctum away from the grid. Flood plains speak of water's rise, while fault lines map the earth's unrest; understanding these signs guides the wise in choosing their ground and fortifying their refuge against nature's inevitable reclaim.

Preparation and Supplies

Amidst the tranquility of off-grid life, vigilance becomes a virtue embodied in the meticulous stockpiling of supplies and the fortification of one's homestead against the tempest's wrath or the earth's upheaval. Water, the most vital of elements stored in abundance, ensures hydration when sources become compromised. Non-perishable foods, their variety safeguarding against malnutrition, stand ready to sustain through weeks of isolation. Tools and materials for repair, from sturdy tarps to versatile duct tape, empower one to mend breaches wrought by wind or quake. Yet, beyond the tangible, the preparation of the mind and spirit for resilience in the face of calamity holds equal importance. Drills that mimic disaster's chaos practiced with solemnity transform panic into purpose, each member of the dwelling becoming a pillar of strength in adversity's tide.

Emergency Communication

In the solitude of the wilderness, where silence reigns, the sudden onset of disaster rends the veil of isolation, thrusting the need for communication into sharp relief. Traditional networks falter under nature's assault, necessitating alternatives that pierce through the storm's howl or the quake's aftermath. Satellite phones, their signals unbound by terrestrial constraints, offer a lifeline to the outside world, their presence in the emergency kit nonnegotiable. Shortwave radios, too, crackle with the voices of distant operators, channels of information, and connection in times when isolation becomes a cage. Pre-arranged signals, shared with neighbors or passing rangers, create a web of awareness, ensuring that even when technology fails, the call for help will find its way through the wilderness to ears that listen.

Shelter and Evacuation

The sanctuary of an off-grid home, nestled in nature's bosom, becomes a fortress against her rage, provided its foundations are laid with foresight. The implementation of architectural and landscaping strategies that rebuff the elements—elevated structures that rise above floodwaters, wind-resistant designs that bend but do not break under the hurricane's fury, seismic retrofitting that holds firm when the earth shakes—enshrines the principle of resilience in wood and stone. Yet, when nature's fury surpasses human defiance, evacuation emerges as the prudent course, a strategic retreat that prioritizes life above all. Routes planned with clarity, free from the threat of falling debris or rising waters, mapped, and memorized, become escape paths from danger. Gathering points, pre-ordained and marked on every map, ensure that even as individuals flee, they converge toward unity and safety.

In this delicate balance between resistance and retreat, the off-grid dweller finds their strength not in the illusion of invulnerability but in the wisdom to yield when the earth reclaims her dominion. The preparedness for natural disasters, a tapestry woven from knowledge, supplies, communication, and strategic mobility, stands as a testament to humanity's resilience. It is a declaration that even in the face of nature's untamed might, there exists a path to safety, to survival, etched in the meticulous planning and indomitable spirit of those who choose to make their lives away from the grid's omnipresent hum.

SELF-DEFENSE TECHNIQUES FOR THE WILDERNESS

In the vast expanse of the wilderness, where the boundary between civilization and the untamed blur, the air hums with a latent tension, a subtle reminder of the unpredictability inherent in such untouched landscapes. Within this domain, the capacity for self-defense emerges not merely as a skill but as an indispensable aspect of survival, a means to navigate potential threats with assurance and poise. The art of self-preservation, thus, pivots on a quartet of principles: situational awareness, the judicious use of non-lethal defense tools, the deployment of physical self-defense maneuvers, and an astute comprehension of the legal landscape governing such actions.

Situational Awareness

At the core of self-defense lies the cultivation of situational awareness, a vigilant observation of one's environment to discern subtle shifts and potential hazards. This heightened state of consciousness, akin to the attunement of wildlife to the whispers of the forest, equips one to preempt and evade threats. It involves a continuous scan of the surroundings, identifying exits, obstacles, and elements that could serve as improvised shields or weapons. Training the senses to detect anomalies in behavior or environment—be it the crackle of underbrush signaling an approaching presence or the uneasy silence that often precedes a storm—fortifies one against surprise, the most perilous element in any confrontation.

Non-lethal Defense Tools

In this arsenal of precaution, non-lethal defense tools occupy a critical niche, offering a means to deter or incapacitate an aggressor without crossing the threshold into lethality. Among these, pepper spray stands out for its efficacy, a compact canister unleashing a potent irritant capable of blinding an assailant, granting precious moments for escape. Similarly, stun devices deliver a jarring shock, disrupting muscle control and, thus, neutralizing a threat temporarily. The mastery of these tools necessitates familiarity with their mechanics, range, and limitations, ensuring they can be deployed swiftly and accurately when seconds count. Regular practice under simulated stress conditions imprints these responses into muscle memory, transforming intention into instinctive action.

Physical Self-Defense

Notwithstanding the utility of tools, there are instances when the immediacy of a threat leaves no recourse but to engage physically. In these moments, a repertoire of basic self-defense moves— strikes to vulnerable areas, breaks from holds, and evasive maneuvers—becomes invaluable. The efficacy of such techniques hinges not on brute strength but on leverage, speed, and the element of surprise. Training with a qualified instructor imparts these skills, melding theory with practice until the body learns to react with precision and confidence. Moreover, this preparation instills an understanding of one's capabilities and limits, enabling a realistic assessment of when to confront and when to conserve energy for escape.

Legal Considerations

Woven through the fabric of self-defense is a thread of legal awareness, a nuanced understanding of the statutes that delineate the boundary between self-preservation and aggression. The legal landscape, varying widely across jurisdictions, dictates the permissible scope of defensive actions, including the use of force and the employment of defense tools. Familiarity with these regulations gained through diligent research or consultation with legal professionals informs decisions in moments of peril, ensuring that the measures taken align with the law's allowances and constraints. This knowledge shields one from the double jeopardy of surviving a physical assault only to confront legal recriminations, anchoring actions within the safe harbor of justified defense.

In the wilderness, where silence speaks, and shadows tell tales, the art of self-defense unfurls as a narrative of empowerment, a dialogue between human resilience and the primal forces of nature. This discourse articulated through the principles of situational awareness, the strategic use of non-lethal defense tools, the application of physical self-defense techniques, and a discerning grasp of legal considerations, crafts a tapestry of preparedness that envelops the sojourner in layers of security. It is within this cocoon of vigilance and readiness that one navigates the wilderness not as a realm of fear but as a landscape of profound connection and indomitable spirit.

As we draw the threads of this discussion to a close, the convergence of these themes—situational awareness, non-lethal tools, physical defense, and legal acuity—emerges not merely as individual strands but as a cohesive weave of survival wisdom. This synthesis, echoing the broader narrative of off-grid resilience, paints a portrait of the wilderness dweller as not merely a survivor but a steward of their own safety and well-being. It is with this empowered stance that we turn our gaze forward, stepping into the next chapter of our journey, where the principles of navigation and exploration beckon, promising new horizons of skill and discovery in the untamed wilds.

NAVIGATING THE UNTAMED: MAP AND COMPASS IN THE WILDERNESS

∞

In a world increasingly reliant on the digital compass of smartphones and GPS devices, the art of traditional navigation whispers tales of the earth, sky, and the magnetic field. This ancient dialogue, spoken through the language of maps and compasses, connects us to the explorers of yore and grounds us in the physical world. It's in this space that we rediscover the primal satisfaction of plotting a course through the wilderness, relying on our senses, intuition, and the steady hands of tried-and-true navigational tools.

MAP READING AND COMPASS SKILLS FOR THE OFF-GRIDDER

Understanding Maps

Topographic maps, with their contours and symbols, offer a multi-dimensional view of the terrain, revealing secrets of the land that might otherwise remain hidden. Reading these maps goes beyond the mere identification of symbols and scales; it's an interpretive dance with geography, where elevation changes become tangible under your fingertips, and water bodies shape the route ahead. Like reading a book, each symbol, contour line, and color variation tells a part of the story, from the whisper of a creek to the roar of a waterfall hidden in the embrace of a valley.

For those uninitiated, a topographic map can seem as cryptic as an ancient manuscript. Yet, with patience and practice, its symbols become familiar friends guiding the way. The scale, often overlooked, is the key to understanding distances, transforming abstract lines into walkable miles. A practical exercise involves plotting a familiar route, perhaps a walk through a local park, using a topographic map. This real-world application solidifies abstract concepts, making the map a trusted guide rather than a mere accessory.

Using a Compass

A compass, in its essence, is a bridge between the map and the physical world, a tool that, when used correctly, ensures the path chosen on paper translates into the correct direction on the ground. The basics of using a compass involve aligning its magnetic needle with magnetic north, a task seemingly simple yet fraught with potential for error if not done with care. Magnetic declination, an often-overlooked factor, varies by location and time, necessitating adjustment for accurate bearings.

A relatable comparison for understanding the compass's role is akin to adjusting the settings on a camera to capture a landscape just as the eye sees it. Without the correct settings, the image captured might look nothing like the intended scene. Similarly, without adjusting for declination, the route followed might lead away from the intended destination.

Orienteering Techniques

Orienteering, a sport born from the marriage of map reading and compass use, offers a dynamic way to hone navigational skills. It's not just a race against time but a test of decision-making, physical endurance, and, most importantly, the ability to read the land through the lens of a map. Local orienteering clubs often host events in parks or natural reserves, providing a structured yet challenging environment to practice these skills. Participating in one of these events, with nothing but a map, compass, and the terrain as your guide, sharpens your ability to make real-time navigational decisions, a skill invaluable in the unpredictable embrace of the wilderness.

Night Navigation

The night sky, a canvas of stars and constellations, serves as a celestial map, guiding travelers long before the invention of the compass or GPS. Navigating by the stars and moon, though seemingly daunting, follows the same principles of orientation and bearing determination as daytime navigation but with celestial bodies as reference points. The North Star, Polaris, offers a fixed point in the northern sky, around which the celestial sphere appears to rotate. Learning to locate Polaris amidst the constellations becomes a crucial skill for night navigation.

One practical tip for night navigation involves using a wristwatch as an improvised compass. By pointing the hour hand at the sun and finding the midpoint between the hour hand and twelve o'clock, one can approximate south in the northern hemisphere during daylight. At night, this method adapts to moonlight with varying degrees of accuracy, offering a rudimentary guide when all else fails.

Wilderness Navigation Checklist

Map Familiarization:

- Identify symbols and scale.
- Practice plotting a familiar route.

Compass Basics:

- Check for magnetic declination in your area.
- Practice aligning the magnetic needle with the magnetic north.

Orienteering Practice:

- Participate in a local orienteering event.
- Focus on decision-making and speed.

Night Navigation:

- Learn to locate Polaris and major constellations.
- Practice the wristwatch method for emergency orientation.

This checklist serves not only as a guide but as a testament to the enduring relevance of traditional navigational skills in an age dominated by digital convenience. It's a call to engage with the great outdoors on its terms, using the tools and knowledge passed down through generations, ensuring that the primal thrill of charting one's course through the wilderness remains accessible to all who seek it.

GPS AND TECH TOOLS FOR WILDERNESS NAVIGATION

In the labyrinth of the untamed, where paths dissolve into the whispering foliage, and the horizon bends with the earth's curvature, the modern wayfarer finds solace and guidance in the invisible threads of satellite signals. The quiet constellation of GPS devices and smartphone apps, invisible yet omnipresent, offers a semblance of certainty in the embrace of the unpredictable. Yet, this reliance on technology, while a beacon in the opaque night, demands a discerning approach, for not all tools are forged alike, and the wilderness cares little for battery life or signal strength.

Choosing GPS Devices

The marketplace, a digital bazaar brimming with gadgets claiming to be the adventurer's ultimate ally, presents a paradox of choice. Here, the selection of a GPS device transcends mere comparison of features; it becomes an assessment of one's very relationship with the wilderness. Devices range from the rudimentary, offering simple coordinates and breadcrumb trails, to the sophisticated, capable of rendering detailed topographic maps and real-time weather updates. The weight of decision leans heavily on the intended use—whether marking waypoints along a serene trail or navigating the treacherous crevasses of ice-clad peaks. Battery life emerges as a critical factor, for the device's prowess is moot if its heart ceases to beat miles away from civilization. Durability and water resistance also command attention, as the elements spare no mercy for electronic companions. In this quest for the perfect device, the wayfarer must balance the desire for functionality with the constraints of weight, cost, and the raw environments they intend to traverse.

Smartphone Apps

The smartphone, that ubiquitous extension of the modern self, morphs into a navigation tool under the canopy of the wild, its screen a window to satellites orbiting in the cold silence of space. Navigation apps, designed to mimic the functionality of dedicated GPS devices, offer a semblance of technological comfort. Yet, their utility in off-grid settings wanes as the signal fades into the ether, reminding users of their inherent limitations. Offline maps become the wayfarer's parchment, downloaded in anticipation of silence from the cellular towers. These apps, while versatile, sip voraciously from the battery's well, urging users to consider power banks as indispensable allies. The wise navigator views these tools with cautious optimism, leveraging their convenience while remaining wary of their dependency on a lifeline of electricity and signal.

Backup Navigation Plans

The lore of seasoned explorers, rich with tales of technology's betrayal at the hands of nature's whims, underscores the imperative of redundancy in navigation. Physical maps and compasses, relics of an older world, regain their stature as indispensable guardians of direction. This duality of digital and analog, a marriage of convenience and reliability, forms the backbone of a robust navigation plan. The map, immune to the failures of batteries and circuits, and the compass, a lodestar unaffected by the absence of satellites, serve as the true north in navigation's constellation. Their presence in the adventurer's pack is not a nod to tradition but a hedge against the fragility of modern tools, a reminder that in the dance of man and nature, one must sometimes lead with the steps of the past.

Battery Management

In the narrative of wilderness exploration, where every moment is a brushstroke on the canvas of experience, the management of battery life in electronic devices transforms into a critical subplot. Strategies to extend the electronic tether to civilization involve not just the judicious use of devices but an understanding of their energy consumption patterns. Power-saving modes dimmed screens, and the selective activation of functions ensure that devices sip rather than gulp from the energy reservoir. Solar chargers, with their promise of harnessing the sun's bounty, offer a semblance of autonomy, transforming light into lifelines. Yet, their efficacy is dictated by the whims of weather and the constraints of travel, often requiring hours for a modest return of power. The astute navigator, recognizing these challenges, weaves a tapestry of conservation and renewal, where devices are but one of many threads in the larger fabric of survival and discovery. In this careful orchestration of technology, the wayfarer finds a balance, ensuring that their journey is marked not by the silence of a dead battery but by the steady pulse of progress toward their destination.

TRACKING AND OBSERVING WILDLIFE SAFELY

Tracking Basics

The silent dialogue between a tracker and the wilderness unveils itself in the delicate impressions left by creatures, great and small. Discerning these signs, a craft refined through patience and acute observation opens a window into the lives of wildlife, their paths woven into the tapestry of the natural world. Each track, be it the padded footprint of a fox or the serpentine trail of a snail, narrates a segment of an ongoing saga, where direction, speed, and behavior etch themselves into the earth. Learning this language initiates one into an ancient fellowship of trackers, where the interpretation of a broken twig or a tuft of fur becomes a key to unlocking the mysteries of animal habits and habitats. This initiation begins with immersion into the environment, eyes attuned to the nuances of disturbance in natural patterns, fingers tracing the edges of imprints to decipher their age and origin. Such dedication transforms the novice into a chronicler of the unseen, bearing witness to the passage of beasts hidden in the veil of the wilderness.

Minimizing Impact

The act of tracking, while a pursuit of knowledge, carries with it the responsibility to tread lightly, ensuring that the quest for understanding does not morph into an intrusion. Strategies for minimizing one's presence hinge on the principles of observation from a distance, utilizing optics to bring the subject closer without stepping into their world. The seasoned tracker becomes a ghost among the foliage, movements measured and silent and breathing tempered to the whispers of the wind. This discipline extends to the selection of observation points, elevated or concealed, where the observer may watch without altering the natural behaviors of wildlife. In this careful balance, the tracker not only learns from but also respects the autonomy of the wild, their study leaving no trace, no scent, no sound to mark their passage.

Safety Precautions

While the wilderness offers tales of beauty and survival, it also harbors narratives of peril, where the roles of observer and observed can swiftly invert. Recognizing the signs of predatory animals becomes a shield, a means to avoid unwittingly stepping into the role of prey. Tracks, scat, and markings on the terrain serve as letters of warning written by the claws and teeth of predators. The knowledge of how to respond should an encounter unfold, straddles the line between standing one's ground and making a strategic retreat, always sideways, eyes locked on the animal, yet never challenging, never running. Such encounters, rare but charged with potential for conflict, underscore the importance of understanding wildlife behavior, the subtle cues that signal curiosity, fear, or aggression. Carrying deterrents, non-lethal but effective, provides an additional layer of security, a reassurance in the pocket or pack that dialogue, not combat, defines human-animal interactions in the wild.

Ethical Considerations

Beneath the surface of tracking and observation lies a foundational ethic, one that respects the sovereignty of wildlife and their right to exist undisturbed. This ethic guides the tracker to consider not only what can be learned but also what should be left alone, where the pursuit of knowledge yields to the higher pursuit of coexistence. It calls for the protection of sensitive habitats, the avoidance of nesting sites, and the preservation of scarce water sources. Furthermore, it champions the sharing of insights gained not for personal acclaim but for the collective understanding and conservation of species and ecosystems. In this way, the tracker becomes not only a student of the wilderness but also its ally and advocate, their actions informed by a reverence for life in all its forms, their legacy inscribed not in the annals of conquest but in the quiet preservation of nature's sanctity. In this communion with the wild, where curiosity is tempered by conscience, the tracker weaves a narrative of harmony, a testament to the possibility of humanity's respectful cohabitation with the myriad forms of life that share this planet.

BUILDING NATURAL SHELTERS: TECHNIQUES AND TIPS

Types of Natural Shelters

In the embrace of the wilderness, the crafting of shelters from the earth's bounty is not merely a skill but a dialogue with nature itself, a way to seek refuge under its canopy without leaving scars on its surface. Lean-tos and debris huts, each with their distinct silhouettes against the backdrop of untamed flora, offer solace and protection with minimal disturbance to the surrounding habitat. The lean-to, with its open face and sloping roof, capitalizes on existing trees or rock formations for support, creating a barrier against prevailing winds while maintaining an openness to the environment. Its counterpart, the debris hut, is an exercise in insulation and camouflage, a cocoon of branches, leaves, and earth that holds the warmth of its occupant like a whispered secret across the forest floor.

Materials and Construction

The selection of materials for these natural shelters follows the principles of sustainability and respect for the land. Fallen branches, leaves, moss, and mud—each element is chosen with consideration for its role not only in the construction of the shelter but in the broader ecosystem. In weaving branches to form the skeleton of a shelter, care is taken to ensure stability and strength, each layer positioned with precision to shed water and buffer against the chill of night air. Leaves and moss, gathered in abundance, serve as a natural insulation stuffed into the framework to create a barrier against the elements. Mud, nature's mortar, seals gaps and reinforces the structure. Its application is an act of patience as layers are built up and smoothed over to weatherproof the shelter.

The act of constructing these shelters is as much about the process as the outcome. It's an immersion into the rhythms of the natural world, where the gathering of materials becomes a meditative practice and the building a test of ingenuity and adaptability. This hands-on experience deepens one's connection to the environment, and each decision and action reflects the impact of human presence in natural spaces.

Weather Considerations

Adapting shelter designs to the whims of weather requires an intimate knowledge of the local climate and an ability to read the signs of impending change. In regions where rainfall is frequent, the slope of the roof and the direction it faces become critical factors designed to channel water away from the interior space. For areas prone to cold snaps, the orientation of the shelter with respect to the sun and the incorporation of a reflective wall or space for a small fire can mean the difference between a frigid night, and one passed in relative comfort. Wind direction, too, informs the positioning of the shelter's opening, minimizing exposure to chilling gusts while allowing for ventilation.

This adaptability extends to the choice of site, where natural features can provide additional protection or resources. A boulder or thicket of bushes may shield against wind or offer material for the shelter's construction. Likewise, proximity to a water source, while convenient, must be balanced against the risk of flooding or attracting wildlife. In this dialogue with the elements, the builder becomes a student of the landscape, learning to harness its offerings while mitigating its dangers.

Practice and Improvisation

Mastery of shelter building is not found in the rigid adherence to blueprints but in the fluidity of improvisation and the willingness to learn through doing. Regular practice in various settings and conditions hones one's ability to construct effective shelters with efficiency and confidence. It's through these repeated exercises that the nuances of different materials and designs reveal themselves, informing future builds and inspiring innovation.

Equally important is the cultivation of an improvisational mindset, where challenges are met with creativity rather than consternation. A snapped branch or a scarcity of leaves becomes an opportunity to experiment with new techniques or materials, expanding one's repertoire of skills. This approach, rooted in flexibility and resourcefulness, prepares one for the unexpected, ensuring that when faced with the need for shelter in an emergency, the response is not panic but purposeful action.

In this exploration of natural shelters, the journey from concept to creation is imbued with lessons that transcend the mere fabrication of a temporary home. It's a path that leads to a deeper understanding and appreciation of the natural world, where each shelter built is a testament to the harmony that can exist between humanity and the environment. Through the types of shelters chosen, the materials and methods of construction employed, the consideration of weather, and the practice of improvisation, one learns not just to survive in the wilderness but to thrive within its embrace, sheltered not only by branches and leaves but by knowledge, skill, and respect for the land.

THE ESSENTIALS OF SAFE AND SUSTAINABLE HUNTING

In the quiet realm where the wilderness whispers secrets of survival and sustenance, the practice of hunting emerges not merely to procure nourishment but as a profound dialogue between humans and nature. This discourse, governed by rules unseen and bonds unspoken, demands a reverence for life, a commitment to the sustainability of the land, and a respect for the creatures that roam it. Within this framework, the hunter navigates a path that honors the past while stewarding the future, ensuring that the legacy of hunting remains untarnished by the passage of time and the imprint of humanity.

Hunting Regulations

The tapestry of hunting laws, woven from threads of conservation science and ethical consideration, serves as a guardian of wildlife populations and their habitats. Adherence to these regulations, which delineate open seasons, permissible methods, and quotas, forms the cornerstone of responsible hunting. Each ordinance, from the specification of caliber to the designation of hunting zones, mirrors an intricate understanding of ecological balance, ensuring that the act of hunting supports the health of ecosystems rather than detracting from it. Familiarity with these laws, acquired through diligent study and engagement with local wildlife authorities, equips the hunter with the knowledge necessary to navigate the legal landscape of the hunt, transforming regulation into a compass that guides ethical and sustainable practice.

Ethical Hunting Practices

Beyond the letter of the law lies the spirit of the hunt, an ethos that transcends regulation, rooting the hunter in a tradition of respect and fairness. The principle of fair chase, advocating for the pursuit under conditions that do not unduly advantage the hunter, stands as a testament to this respect, challenging the hunter to engage with the quarry on terms that honor its instincts and prowess. This respect extends to the moment of harvest, where a quick and humane end is sought, minimizing suffering, and honoring the life taken. Within this context, the hunter emerges not as a conqueror but as a participant in the cycle of life, their actions guided by a deep-seated reverence for the creature and the contribution it makes to the hunter's survival.

Safety Protocols

The wielding of weapons, be they bows or firearms, imbues the hunt with an inherent risk, a variable that demands rigorous control through disciplined safety protocols. The handling of firearms, charged with the potential for harm, follows strict guidelines—muzzles pointed away from companions, fingers resting outside the trigger guard until the moment of intent, and the identification of the target and what lies beyond it. Communication, too, plays a pivotal role, a thread that binds the hunting party in a web of awareness, ensuring that each member is accounted for and that their positions are known. This discipline instilled through education and practice, transforms the hunt from an endeavor fraught with danger into a practice marked by mindfulness and mutual care, where safety becomes the pulse that underpins every action.

Processing and Preservation

The culmination of the hunt, the transition from chase to table, involves skills that bridge tradition and necessity. The field dressing of game, an act as ancient as hunting itself, demands precision and understanding, careful separation of flesh from fur, of nourishment from nature's return. This initial step, conducted with an eye toward cleanliness and efficiency, prevents spoilage and prepares the meat for the journey home. The subsequent processing, whether in the field or the kitchen, transforms the harvest into forms suited for consumption and storage—cuts of meat, carefully butchered, and portions preserved through smoking, curing, or freezing. Each technique, rooted in the ancestral knowledge of hunters who came before, ensures that not a morsel of the gift provided by the hunt goes to waste, honoring the life taken by extending its nourishment to sustain others.

In the unfolding narrative of hunting within the embrace of the wild, these principles—adherence to regulations, ethical practices, safety protocols, and the respectful processing and preservation of the game—serve as chapters in a story of coexistence. They paint a portrait of the hunter as both a steward of the land and a participant in its ancient rhythms, where the act of hunting remains intertwined with the fabric of survival, bound by the threads of ethical consideration, legal adherence, and a deep-seated respect for the natural world. This narrative, devoid of a definitive end, continues with each hunter who chooses to step into the wilderness, guided by these tenets, ensuring that the legacy of hunting endures as a practice of sustainability, respect, and reverence for life in its myriad forms.

WILDERNESS PHOTOGRAPHY: CAPTURING YOUR OFF-GRID LIFE

In the vast expanse where the untamed whispers its ancient stories, the lens of a camera becomes a vessel, capturing fleeting moments and crystallizing them into tangible memories. This practice of wilderness photography, more than a mere collection of images, is a profound connection to the natural world, a dialogue between the observer and the observed, mediated through the quiet click of a shutter. For the off-grid enthusiast, it offers a unique means to document the journey, celebrate the beauty of nature, and share a narrative that might inspire conservation and a deeper respect for our planet.

Choosing Equipment

Navigating the myriad options for cameras and accessories demands a discerning eye, one that can sift through the glittering allure of new gadgets to find tools that align with the rigors and requirements of wilderness photography. The decision between a DSLR, with its interchangeable lenses and high-quality images, and a compact mirrorless camera, lighter and less obtrusive in the quiet of the wild, hinges on a balance of image quality, weight, and the photographer's intentions. Lenses, those eyes through which the camera sees the world, require thoughtful selection; a versatile zoom lens for landscapes and a faster prime lens for capturing wildlife in motion become staples in the photographer's pack. Beyond the camera itself, accessories like tripods for stability in uneven terrain, filters to manage light and color, as well as protective cases to shield against the elements are crucial. These tools, when chosen with an understanding of their function and the environment they will be used in, become extensions of the photographer's vision, enabling the capture of images that resonate with the essence of wilderness life.

Photography Techniques

With equipment in hand, the technique becomes the soul of wilderness photography, the element that breathes life into images. Patience is paramount; it's the currency spent waiting for the perfect light as dawn breaks over a mountain ridge or for a shy creature to reveal itself from the thicket. Composition, the thoughtful arrangement of elements within the frame, follows principles that guide the eye and evoke emotion, yet knows when to break the rules to capture the untamed spirit of the wild. The mastery of exposure, balancing aperture, shutter speed, and ISO translates the dynamic range of natural light into images that shimmer with realism or moan with moodiness. For those candid moments, the unguarded laughter around a campfire or the serene contemplation of a sunset, a readiness to capture the spontaneous ensures that the heart of off-grid life is preserved, one click at a time.

Respecting Nature

This endeavor, while a celebration of the wilderness, carries with it a responsibility to tread lightly, ensuring that the quest for the perfect shot does not become an imposition on the natural world. Guidelines for respectful photography emphasize distance, utilizing zoom lenses to capture wildlife without intrusion into their space or altering their behavior. The avoidance of baiting or calls that stress animals for the sake of a photo is a testament to the photographer's integrity. Equally, the practice of "leave no trace" extends to photography, where landscapes are left as they were found, untouched by the photographer's presence. In adhering to these principles, wilderness photography becomes an act of reverence, a homage to the beauty and fragility of nature.

Sharing Your Story

The images captured, each a frozen note in the symphony of off-grid life, find their purpose when shared. Social media platforms offer a stage, a space where these visual narratives can unfold, reaching eyes and hearts across the globe. But, beyond mere exhibition, the sharing of wilderness photography serves a higher calling, advocating for the preservation of natural spaces and the creatures that inhabit them. Blogs and photo essays weave images and words into compelling calls to action, inviting others to not only admire the beauty of the wild but to engage in efforts to protect it. Exhibitions, whether in local galleries or community centers, bring the wilderness to those who might never venture into it, bridging the gap between urban life and the natural world. Through these channels, the off-grid photographer becomes a storyteller, an ambassador of the wild, fostering appreciation, respect, and a collective commitment to conservation.

As we encapsulate the essence of wilderness photography, from the meticulous selection of equipment and the honing of technique to the ethical considerations that guide our practice and the sharing of our visual narratives, we touch upon something fundamental. This practice, more than a mere hobby or profession, is a bridge between humanity and the natural world, a medium through which we communicate our reverence, our concerns, and our hopes for the planet. It's a reminder that beauty exists in the wild spaces, in the untamed and the untouched, and that we hold the power, through the images we capture and share, to influence how these spaces are treated by current and future generations. Moving forward, let us carry these reflections as a beacon, guiding our interactions with the natural world, whether through the lens of a camera or the eyes of our soul.

LIVING IN HARMONY:
SUSTAINING MENTAL AND COMMUNITY HEALTH OFF-GRID

In the vast canvas of wilderness, where the only echoes are those of nature's breath and one's own thoughts, the specter of isolation can cast a long shadow. Here, amidst the undulating hills and whispering winds, the mind seeks refuge not just from the elements but from the solitude that envelops it. This solitude, while a balm to the weary spirit, can also morph into a chasm of isolation, challenging one's mental fortitude. It is within this delicate balance that strategies for mental health and community involvement become not just beneficial but vital, weaving a tapestry of support and engagement that sustains the soul.

OVERCOMING ISOLATION: STRATEGIES FOR MENTAL HEALTH

Community Involvement

In the solace of the off-grid life, the draw of the community becomes a beacon, guiding toward connection and belonging. Engaging with local communities, whether through shared projects, local markets, or communal gatherings, bridges the gap between solitude and isolation. Online forums serve as a digital campfire around which experiences, challenges, and triumphs are shared, forging bonds that transcend physical distances. This collective engagement, reminiscent of the communal living of our ancestors, rekindles a sense of purpose and belonging, anchoring the individual in a network of shared human experiences.

In a small village, the tradition of weekly gatherings at the community center, where stories and produce are exchanged, exemplifies this principle. Here, connections are nurtured, loneliness abates, and the fabric of the community tightens, providing a safety net against the void of isolation.

Routine and Hobbies

Structure and passion intertwine to form a bulwark against the tides of loneliness. Establishing a daily routine imbues life with rhythm and predictability, countering the erratic nature of wilderness living. Hobbies and passions act as conduits for expression and exploration, tethering the mind to joy and curiosity. Gardening, crafting, or writing not only fills the hours but also deepens the connection with one's surroundings and inner self. This structured engagement, much like the predictable cycles of nature, brings a comforting cadence to off-grid life, transforming empty hours into reservoirs of growth and creativity.

Mental Health Practices

Mindfulness, meditation, and exercise emerge as pillars supporting the edifice of mental well-being. Mindfulness grounds one in the present amidst the beauty and tranquility of the wilderness, fostering a deep appreciation for the now. Meditation, whether seated beneath the canopy of stars or walking through a meadow at dawn, declutters the mind, silencing the whispers of solitude. Exercise, in harmony with nature's expanse, strengthens both body and spirit, releasing the endorphins that brighten mood and outlook. This triad, when practiced with consistency, constructs a fortress of well-being around the individual, shielding against the specters of depression and anxiety.

Seeking Support

The acknowledgment that some chasms are too wide to bridge alone marks a pivotal step toward sustaining mental health. Professional help sought in times of prolonged isolation or depression offers a lifeline back to equilibrium. Teletherapy, a modern boon, breaks down the barriers of distance, providing access to guidance and support from the sanctity of one's wilderness retreat. This proactive approach, recognizing when external help is needed, underscores the strength in vulnerability, a testament to the human capacity to seek and find light, even in the shadow of isolation.

Overcoming Isolation Checklist

Community Engagement:

- Attend local community gatherings or markets.
- Participate in online forums or social media groups related to off-grid living.

Routine and Hobbies:

- Establish a daily routine that includes time outdoors.
- Dedicate time to hobbies that connect you with nature and your passions.

Mental Health Practices:

- Practice mindfulness daily, focusing on the beauty of your surroundings.
- Incorporate meditation and exercise into your routine to enhance mental clarity and mood.

Seeking Support:

- Identify signs of prolonged isolation or depression.
- Explore teletherapy options for professional mental health support.

This checklist, a beacon in the vastness of off-grid living, offers practical steps toward nurturing mental health and community connections. It serves as a reminder that while the wilderness offers a retreat from the world, sustaining mental well-being requires a bridge back to the essence of our shared humanity—connection, purpose, and support.

BUILDING AN OFF-GRID COMMUNITY: NETWORKING AND SUPPORT

In the vast tapestry of off-grid living, woven from threads of resilience, independence, and a profound connection to the natural world, the communities we create, and nurture stand as pillars of strength. These communities, whether rooted in the physical proximity of shared land or the digital expanse of the internet, offer havens of knowledge, support, and shared experiences. They serve as lighthouses, guiding us through the fog of isolation and uncertainty that can sometimes shroud the off-grid journey.

Community Creation

The genesis of an off-grid community, whether finding oneself within the embrace of an existing collective or sowing the seeds for a new aggregation, demands both vision and pragmatism. For those seeking to weave their lives into the fabric of established communities, the journey begins with immersion, engaging in the rhythms and rituals of these groups, contributing one's unique skills, and learning from the communal pool of knowledge. This immersion fosters bonds, knitting newcomers into the communal quilt with threads of trust and mutual respect.

Conversely, the establishment of a new community, a beacon for like-minded souls seeking refuge from the cacophony of conventional existence, requires a foundation laid upon shared values and common goals. The initial step, often the most daunting, involves outreach, casting a net through channels bathed in the ethos of sustainability and self-reliance. Workshops, forums, and social media platforms dedicated to the nuances of off-grid living serve as fertile ground for these seeds of community, drawing together individuals whose hearts beat in sync with the rhythms of the earth.

Shared Resources and Knowledge

The lifeblood of any community flows from the wellspring of shared resources and collective wisdom. In the context of off-grid living, this sharing transcends the mere exchange of goods or labor; it becomes an intricate dance of give and take, where the currency is not material but knowledge, experience, and time. Tool libraries, seed exchanges, and cooperative builds become tangible expressions of this ethos, each member contributing to the communal pot from which all may draw. Workshops on solar installation, water harvesting, or permaculture design, led by members who have trodden these paths, spread knowledge like wildfire, igniting sparks of innovation and self-sufficiency across the community.

This collective resource pool, however, thrives only with the nourishment of transparency and reciprocity. Trust, the mortar holding together the bricks of shared endeavors, grows from the soil of open communication and equitable contribution, ensuring that each member, regardless of their tenure in the community, feels valued and heard.

Community Events

The weaving of social fabric, tight and resilient, finds its rhythm in the organization of community events and gatherings. These occasions, marked by the sharing of food, stories, and laughter, serve as the heartbeat of the community, a tangible expression of unity and belonging. Seasonal celebrations mark the cycles of planting and harvest, the solstices, and equinoxes, rooting the community in the natural calendar and aligning human endeavors with the ebb and flow of the natural world.

More than mere social engagements, these events act as catalysts for collaboration, sparking conversations that might birth new projects or solve communal challenges. They also serve as gateways for outsiders, offering a glimpse into the ethos and operations of the community, potentially drawing new members into the fold. The planning and execution of these gatherings, democratic and inclusive, reflect the collective spirit, ensuring that each voice finds representation in the tapestry of communal life.

Online Platforms

In an era where digital threads weave into the fabric of daily existence, online platforms emerge as vital tools in the expansion and deepening of off-grid communities. Virtual forums and social media groups offer spaces where geographical boundaries dissolve, allowing ideas, advice, and support to flow freely among individuals scattered across the globe. These digital gatherings become lifelines, connecting those in remote locales with a global community of peers navigating similar paths of sustainability and self-reliance.

Beyond the exchange of ideas, these platforms facilitate the sharing of resources in broader, more impactful ways. Crowdfunding campaigns for communal projects, virtual marketplaces for the exchange of goods and services, and collaborative online workshops extend the reach of the community, embedding it within a global network of off-grid and sustainable living advocates. This digital extension does not dilute the essence of the community but enriches it, drawing in diverse perspectives and experiences that strengthen the collective resolve and broaden the horizons of what is possible in off-grid living.

In navigating the creation and nurturing of off-grid communities, one engages in the act of co-creation, where the contributions of each member weave into a vibrant tapestry of support, learning, and shared experiences. This communal endeavor, grounded in the principles of reciprocity, sustainability, and mutual respect, stands as a testament to the enduring human capacity for adaptation, collaboration, and growth. Through the channels of physical proximity and digital connection, these communities offer a blueprint for a future where independence is balanced with interdependence and self-reliance is enriched by collective wisdom.

EDUCATION OFF-GRID: LEARNING AND TEACHING IN THE WILDERNESS

Amidst the verdant embrace of the wilderness, where the boundaries of traditional classrooms blur into the horizon, lies an untapped reservoir of knowledge ripe for exploration through alternative education models. The concept of imparting wisdom in this setting transcends conventional pedagogies, embracing a fusion of homeschooling, unschooling, and community-based education models that cater to the unique rhythms of off-grid living. This approach not only nurtures the intellect but also fortifies the soul, crafting individuals who are not merely scholars of textbooks but stewards of the earth.

Alternative Education Models

The journey into homeschooling within the wilderness unfurls as a path lined with the richness of tailored curriculums that dance to the unique tune of each child's curiosity and pace. Here, subjects are not confined to the pages of a book but are alive in the rustling of leaves, the patterns of the stars, and the geometry of spider webs. Unschooling, with its radical trust in the child's natural inclination toward learning, flourishes in this environment. It operates on the principle that education is not a forced endeavor but a spontaneous exploration of the world. Meanwhile, community-based education models thrive on the collective wisdom of the off-grid enclave, where knowledge is a communal feast to which everyone contributes. Skills crucial for sustainable living, from gardening to renewable energy management, are passed down through generations, ensuring that each member, young or old, is both a teacher and a student in the vast classroom of the wilderness.

Skill-sharing

In the heart of the wilderness, where every day is a lesson in survival and sustainability, skill-sharing emerges as a vital thread that binds the community together. Organizing sessions where knowledge flows freely among individuals transforms the abstract concept of education into a tangible exchange of wisdom. A seasoned forager revealing the secrets of edible mushrooms, a carpenter sharing the intricacies of building with natural materials, or a solar technician demystifying the workings of photovoltaic cells—these gatherings become crucibles of learning. The beauty of this approach lies in its reciprocity; everyone has something to teach and something to learn, creating a culture of mutual improvement and respect for diverse skills.

Learning from Nature

Nature, in its infinite wisdom, offers lessons that no textbook can encapsulate. Direct interaction with the environment, where the subtle language of the earth and its inhabitants becomes a subject of study, cultivates an intimate understanding of the world. This pedagogy encourages not just observation but immersion, where learning is a sensory experience. Tracking animals, identifying plants, understanding weather patterns, and recognizing the interconnectedness of ecosystems unfold as chapters in an ever-evolving curriculum taught by the wilderness itself. Such education fosters not only a deep appreciation for the natural world but also a profound sense of responsibility toward its preservation.

Educational Resources

Complementing the hands-on learning experiences that the wilderness affords, a wealth of online and library resources stands ready to deepen this educational journey. Digital platforms offer courses, documentaries, and interactive tools that bridge the gap between remote living and global knowledge bases. Libraries, too, play a crucial role, their collections providing a tangible connection to the broader human experience and the cumulative wisdom of civilizations. These resources, when woven into the fabric of off-grid education, enrich the learning landscape, offering perspectives and insights that enhance the understanding gleaned from the living classroom of the wilderness.

In this fusion of alternative education models, skill-sharing, direct lessons from nature, and the strategic use of educational resources, a new paradigm of learning emerges. It's one that honors the rhythms of the natural world and the innate curiosity of the human spirit, crafting individuals deeply rooted in their environment and equipped with the knowledge and skills to navigate the complexities of the modern world. This approach to education, holistic and integrative, ensures that the legacy of off-grid living extends beyond mere survival, nurturing minds that are as resilient as they are enlightened, ready to face the challenges of tomorrow with wisdom born from the timeless teachings of the wilderness.

BALANCING SOLITUDE AND SOCIAL LIFE IN THE WILDERNESS

In the heart of vast wildernesses, where silence offers a symphony of its own and the horizon stretches beyond the confines of imagination, solitude becomes a revered companion. This solitude, far from the cacophony of urban sprawl, harbors a purity that invites introspection and self-discovery. Yet, within its embrace, the human spirit whispers ancient communal bonds, urging a delicate dance between the solace of isolation and the warmth of social connection. Here, the off-gridder navigates a path that honors both the quietude of the wild and the innate yearning for human interaction, crafting a life that resonates with the harmonies of solitude and society.

Embracing Solitude

In solitude, one finds a mirror reflecting the contours of the soul, each moment of quietude a step deeper into the realms of self-awareness. This journey inward is not a retreat but an exploration, where the whispers of the mind and the cadences of the heart compose a narrative of personal growth. The wilderness, with its unscripted landscapes and untamed beauty, serves as a backdrop to this introspection, its vastness a canvas for the brushstrokes of self-realization. Engaging in this solitude requires an acceptance of the wilderness not just as a physical space but as a spiritual sanctuary, where the absence of noise reveals the music of one's inner world.

Socializing Strategically

Yet, as roots intertwine with the earth, so does the human spirit seek connection with its kin. Strategic socializing, a deliberate weaving of social threads into the fabric of off-grid life, ensures that solitude does not harden into isolation. Visits to neighboring settlements or planned gatherings with fellow wilderness dwellers transform into pilgrimages of social replenishment. These interactions, marked not by their frequency but by their depth and sincerity, rekindle communal bonds, reminding one that society thrives not on proximity but on shared experiences and mutual understanding. In these moments, stories flow like rivers, laughter rises like a bonfire's sparks, and the essence of community revives, nourishing the soul.

Technology for Connection

In the tapestry of modern existence, technology weaves a thread that binds distant hearts, its pulse beating across the void. For those nestled in nature's embrace, technology serves not as a tether to old lives but as a bridge to beloved faces and voices. Video calls transform screens into windows, through which smiles are shared across miles, and messages ferry thoughts and affections, swift as the falcon's flight. Yet, this embrace of digital connectivity walks hand in hand with mindfulness, ensuring that screens illuminate but do not overshadow the luminance of the stars above. In this judicious use of technology, the off-grid life finds balance, staying woven into the fabric of wider social circles while remaining anchored in the tranquility of the wild.

Community Roles

Within the microcosm of off-grid and local communities, each member casts a stone into the mosaic of communal life, their roles as varied as the hues of the wilderness at dusk. Identifying one's place in this intricate design fosters a sense of belonging, a recognition that each contribution, no matter its scale, enriches the collective. Some may find their niche in the guardianship of nature, leading efforts to conserve and protect. Others might lend their voices to the chorus of education, sharing knowledge and skills that underpin the sustainability of off-grid living. Some people's culinary endeavors or craftsmanship in art can become a source of communal joy and pride. In assuming these roles, individuals weave their threads into the communal tapestry, each pattern unique yet part of a greater whole. This recognition of roles not only cements a sense of purpose but also celebrates the diversity of talents and passions that thrive within the bosom of off-grid communities.

In navigating the realms of solitude and social life within the embrace of the wilderness, the off-gridder crafts a symphony of existence that honors the depths of introspection and the heights of communal connection. This delicate equilibrium, maintained through the conscious embrace of solitude, strategic socializing, the judicious use of technology, and the active assumption of communal roles, composes a life of rich textures and harmonies. In this balance, the wilderness becomes not just a place of refuge but a home where the spirit, nourished by quiet and the community alike, flourishes.

THE ROLE OF PETS AND ANIMALS IN OFF-GRID LIVING

In the realm where the grid's reach fades into the embrace of untamed landscapes, animals, both domestic and wild, assume roles far beyond their traditional ones as companions or subjects of idyllic admiration. They become integral threads in the fabric of off-grid life, each strand representing a symbiotic relationship that enriches human existence with a depth of companionship, responsibility, sustainability, and harmony with nature that city life seldom affords.

Companionship

The silent pact of companionship between humans and their pets finds a profound expression in the solitude of off-grid settings. Here, the presence of a dog, with its unflagging loyalty and boundless joy, or a cat, with its serene independence and comforting purrs, transcends mere pet ownership. These animals become confidants, their silent understanding offering solace in moments of solitude, their antics a source of laughter that echoes against the backdrop of the wilderness. This bond, nurtured in the expanse of nature, grows stronger with each shared dawn and dusk, each walk through the woods or quiet evening by the fire. It is a companionship that does not speak in words but in the language of shared experiences and unconditional acceptance, a balm for the soul that soothes the pangs of isolation inherent to life off the beaten path.

Responsibility and Care

With the joy of animal companionship comes the gravity of responsibility, a duty that off-grid living amplifies. The care of animals in this context demands not only the provision of food, water, and shelter but also a keen awareness of their well-being in an environment that offers both freedom and unforeseen hazards. Vaccinations, regular health checks, and preventive measures against local wildlife threats become part of the rhythm of off-grid routines. This stewardship extends to ensuring that pets and farm animals do not disrupt the delicate ecological balance, teaching them to coexist with native species without predation or harassment. In this, the off-gridder learns the weight of caring for another life, a responsibility that teaches planning, empathy, and the joy of seeing animals thrive in a setting that respects their natural behaviors.

Integrating Animals into Sustainability

Beyond companionship, animals contribute significantly to the sustainability of off-grid homesteads, their roles ingeniously intertwined with the cycles of nature. Chickens, with their tireless foraging, provide natural pest control while offering eggs, a renewable source of nutrition. Goats and sheep, in their grazing, manage the underbrush, reducing fire hazards and improving pasture health. Even the waste from these animals becomes a resource, enriching compost piles that, in turn, nourish vegetable gardens and fruit trees. This integration of animals into the homestead's ecological cycles exemplifies a permaculture approach, where every element serves multiple purposes, enhancing the self-sufficiency and sustainability of off-grid living. It is a harmonious interplay that underscores the principle of giving back to the land that sustains a lesson in the mutual benefits of symbiotic relationships.

Wildlife Coexistence

The tapestry of off-grid living is not woven solely of human, pet, and farm animal interactions but includes the vital threads of local wildlife, a constant reminder of the wildness that envelops it. Coexisting with these native inhabitants requires an understanding of their needs and behaviors, an acknowledgment that the land is shared, and that every effort must be made to minimize human impact. This coexistence is nurtured through practices like securing food sources to prevent attracting wildlife to living areas, maintaining a respectful distance to observe without disturbing, and preserving natural habitats by minimizing land alteration. Such practices foster an environment where wildlife can thrive alongside human habitation, contributing to biodiversity and offering the immeasurable richness of living near nature's untamed beauty. In this reciprocal relationship, the off-gridder becomes not an intruder but a guardian of the land, ensuring that their presence adds to rather than detracts from the ecological tapestry of their wilderness home.

In the heart of off-grid living, where the boundaries between human and animal, domestic and wild, blur, life assumes a richness textured with the companionship of pets, the responsibility of care, the sustainability of integrating animals into homestead cycles, and the harmony of coexisting with wildlife. This interwoven existence, enriched by the contributions of each being, offers lessons in empathy, sustainability, and the profound interconnectedness of all life. It is a living mosaic, vibrant with the colors of shared existence and mutual respect, a testament to the possibility of a life lived in deep harmony with the natural world.

HOSTING WORKSHOPS AND TOURS: SHARING YOUR OFF-GRID EXPERIENCE

In the heart of a wilderness embraced by those who step away from the mechanical hum of society, the act of sharing one's practices through workshops and tours becomes a rich tapestry of education and inspiration. These gatherings, illuminated by the soft glow of shared knowledge, offer a window into the possibilities of a life intertwined with nature's rhythms, where sustainability is not an abstract ideal but a lived reality.

Workshop Planning

Crafting workshops that resonate require a melding of passion with pedagogy, where the subjects offered mirror both the expertise of the host and the curiosity of the community. The initial step involves a meticulous mapping of topics, from the simplicity of composting to the complexities of solar energy systems, each chosen for its relevance and potential to empower participants. Following this, the logistics of space, whether within the embrace of a forest clearing or the warmth of a barn converted into a communal learning space, demand attention, ensuring accessibility and harmony with the subjects taught.

Materials gathered not from the sterile aisles of stores but from the bounty of the land and the ingenuity of recycling underscore the workshops' ethos. Promotion, woven through the channels of local bulletins and digital networks, calls out to those hungry for knowledge, while registration systems, simple yet efficient, capture burgeoning interest. In this orchestration of details, the workshop transcends mere instruction, becoming a crucible of transformation where skills are not just learned but absorbed into the very fabric of participants' lives.

Tour Experiences

Offering tours of one's off-grid setup invites the curious to step into a world where sustainability breathes through every structure and system. These tours, curated with an eye for both the miraculous and the mundane, peel back the veil on off-grid living, revealing the interplay of rainwater harvesting tanks, solar panels, wind turbines, and permaculture gardens. Guides, fluent in the language of sustainability, weave stories that highlight not just the how but the why, engaging visitors in a dialogue that challenges preconceptions and kindles aspirations.

Safety, a silent guardian of experience, ensures that the wonder of discovery is never marred by preventable mishaps. Accessibility, too, forms a core consideration, inviting a diversity of visitors to witness the harmony of off-grid life. In the reflection of visitors' wide-eyed wonder, the off-grid host finds a mirror to their own journey, a reminder of the first steps taken on this path less traveled.

Online Content

In the digital realm, where ideas travel at the speed of light, blogs, videos, and podcasts serve as beacons, guiding global audiences toward the light of sustainability and self-sufficiency. Crafting content that captivates demands not just a command of the medium but an authenticity of voice, where personal anecdotes and failures shared with humility stand shoulder to shoulder with triumphs. Videos, with their visual allure, transport viewers into the heart of the wilderness, offering a lens through which the beauty and challenges of off-grid living are vividly experienced. Podcasts, intimate and conversational, invite listeners into the fold, discussions illuminating the nuances of a life entwined with nature.

In this endeavor, consistency becomes a companion, ensuring that the thread of narrative continues to unspool, drawing audiences deeper into the journey. Engagement, the reciprocity of digital communication, nurtures a community of followers, their comments and questions weaving a tapestry of collective curiosity and learning.

Community Engagement

The ultimate confluence of workshops, tours, and digital narratives lies in their capacity to foster a community, both local and global, united by a shared passion for sustainability. This engagement, rich in dialogue and diversity, sows the seeds for a broader movement toward living in harmony with the earth. Collaborations, born from the crossing of paths at a workshop or a comment on a blog post, flourish into projects that amplify the impact of individual efforts.

In these gatherings, virtual and physical, the off-grid lifestyle finds its chorus, a multitude of voices singing a shared song of hope, innovation, and resilience. It is here, in the exchange of knowledge and the celebration of sustainable living, that a vision of a better world takes root, nurtured by the collective wisdom and action of a community drawn together by the desire to tread lightly upon the earth.

As we weave the threads of sharing our off-grid experiences through workshops, tours, and the digital sphere, we craft a narrative that extends beyond the confines of our immediate surroundings. This sharing becomes a beacon, illuminating the path for others inspired by the vision of a sustainable, harmonious existence with nature. It reaffirms our commitment not only to the lifestyle we have chosen but to the broader mission of fostering a community united in its pursuit of sustainability. In this journey of sharing and engagement, we find not just fulfillment in our own endeavors but the joy of seeing the seeds of inspiration take root in the hearts and minds of others, promising a future where living off-grid is not an outlier but a shared aspiration.

Thus, as we transition from the exploration of community and sharing to the realms of personal growth and environmental stewardship, we carry forward the lessons learned, ready to delve deeper into the symbiotic relationship between human aspiration and the natural world.

INNOVATING HARMONY: OFF-GRID LIVING'S NEW FRONTIER

A seed, when planted in fertile soil, watered, and given ample sunlight, does not merely grow; it transforms. Similarly, off-grid living, rooted in the principles of self-sufficiency and sustainability, evolves through innovation. This evolution, driven by technological advancements and a deep understanding of traditional methods, is not a departure from its essence but an expansion, a flowering of potential that reaches toward efficiency and harmony with the natural world.

THE ROLE OF INNOVATION IN OFF-GRID LIVING

Technological Advancements

The canvas of off-grid living, once painted with broad strokes of manual labor and rudimentary tools, now sees the infusion of technology, bringing with it a palette of efficiency and accessibility. Solar panels, once bulky and inefficient, now boast lightweight, flexible designs with higher energy conversion rates. Their integration into off-grid systems has transitioned from an ambitious endeavor to a practical step toward energy independence. Similarly, water purification technologies have advanced from simple filtration to sophisticated systems capable of extracting clean water from the air, an innovation akin to drawing blood from a stone. This leap in technological capabilities does not eclipse the essence of off-grid living but enhances its feasibility, making sustainable living not just a choice for the rugged but an attainable lifestyle for many.

Adapting Traditional Methods

The wisdom of traditional off-grid methods, honed over generations, finds new expression through innovation. Composting toilets, an ancient solution to the problem of waste management, have seen a renaissance through designs that not only minimize odor and pathogens but also convert human waste into a resource for soil enrichment. The adaptation of these methods, blending time-tested wisdom with modern engineering, creates solutions that honor the past while addressing present-day sustainability challenges. This approach, where innovation walks hand in hand with tradition, ensures that the evolution of off-grid living respects its roots while striving for greater efficiency and environmental harmony.

Research and Development

Innovation in off-grid living thrives on a bedrock of continuous research and development. Academic institutions and independent researchers explore new materials for building insulation, study the impacts of micro-hydro systems on local ecosystems, and develop off-grid refrigeration technologies that operate without electricity. This pursuit of knowledge, driven by curiosity and a commitment to sustainability, expands the boundaries of what is possible in off-grid living. It is a reminder that progress in this field is not measured solely by advancements in technology but by our deepening understanding of how-to live-in harmony with the natural world.

Collaborations

The fusion of off-gridders, technologists, and environmental scientists in collaborative endeavors marks a promising horizon for innovation in sustainable living. These partnerships, grounded in mutual respect for diverse expertise, catalyze breakthroughs that no single discipline could achieve alone. A project that pairs solar engineers with permaculture experts to create integrated energy and food production systems exemplifies this collaborative spirit. Here, the sharing of knowledge and resources not only leads to innovative solutions but also fosters a sense of community among those dedicated to the advancement of off-grid living.

Innovation Checklist

- **Evaluate Energy Systems:** Assess current energy setup for efficiency and explore advancements in solar, wind, and micro-hydro technologies.
- **Revitalize Traditional Methods:** Identify traditional off-grid practices in need of innovation; consider modern composting solutions or water purification systems.
- **Engage in Research:** Stay informed about the latest studies and developments in sustainable living practices and technologies.
- **Seek Collaborations:** Connect with experts in technology, environmental science, and traditional off-grid methods to drive innovation in your off-grid setup.

This checklist serves as a guide for those navigating the evolving landscape of off-grid living, encouraging a proactive approach to innovation that balances technological advancement with traditional wisdom. It underscores the importance of continuous learning, collaboration, and adaptation in the pursuit of a sustainable, harmonious existence with the natural world.

Innovation in off-grid living is not a departure from its foundational principles but an expansion, a flowering of potential that embraces both the wisdom of tradition and the advancements of modern technology. This evolution, driven by research, development, and collaboration, ensures that off-grid living remains not only a viable alternative to conventional lifestyles but a leading edge of sustainable human habitation. As we explore new technologies, adapt traditional methods and foster collaborations, we plant the seeds for a future where living off the grid is accessible, efficient, and in harmony with the earth's rhythms.

EMERGING TECHNOLOGIES IN RENEWABLE ENERGY

In a world where whispers of innovation breathe life into the dormant and the static, renewable energy technology stands at the forefront, a beacon guiding toward a future where dependence on non-renewable sources becomes a relic of the past. This relentless pursuit of efficiency and sustainability has birthed advancements that not only redefine the boundaries of possibility but also promise a renaissance in the way we harness, store, and utilize energy in off-grid living scenarios.

Solar Power Innovations

The realm of solar power, once limited by bulky installations and modest efficiency, now flourishes with innovations that challenge these constraints, heralding a new era of accessibility and effectiveness. Perovskite solar cells, emerging from the confluence of material science and photovoltaic research, stand poised to revolutionize solar energy capture with their promise of higher efficiency rates and lower production costs. Unlike their silicon counterparts, these cells thrive on a synthesis process that allows for thinner, more flexible applications, envisioning a future where solar energy capture integrates seamlessly into the fabric of everyday life, from windows to vehicle surfaces.

Beyond the cell itself, tracking systems have evolved, employing machine learning algorithms to predict and adapt to weather conditions, optimizing energy capture in real-time. This synergy between predictive technology and mechanical precision ensures that each ray of sunlight, from the gentle dawn to the golden hues of dusk, contributes to the energy reservoir, minimizing waste and maximizing potential.

Wind and Hydropower

Advances in small-scale wind and hydropower systems have redefined their roles in off-grid energy solutions, transforming these once cumbersome installations into compact, efficient, and adaptable units. Vertical-axis wind turbines, with their reduced footprint and ability to capture wind from multiple directions, offer a solution that fits the spatial and aesthetic demands of off-grid living without compromising on power generation. Their design, a fusion of elegance and engineering, allows for placement closer to living spaces, reducing transmission losses, and blending with the natural and built environment.

Micro-hydropower, tapping into the latent energy of flowing water, has seen similar strides in innovation. Systems now incorporate modular designs that simplify installation and maintenance, making them suitable for a wider range of water sources, from small streams to seasonal rivulets. The integration of smart monitoring technologies ensures optimal performance, adjusting to variations in water flow and quality, safeguarding both the system and the aquatic ecosystem from which it draws power.

Energy Storage

The Achilles' heel of renewable energy—its intermittent—finds a formidable opponent in the latest breakthroughs in energy storage solutions. Lithium-ion batteries, long hailed for their high energy density and long-life cycles, are giving way to alternatives like solid-state and flow batteries. These newcomers promise enhanced not only safety and environmental friendliness but also a leap in storage capacity and discharge rates, enabling off-gridders to store more energy for longer periods, thereby bridging the gap between supply and demand with unprecedented efficiency.

Moreover, the exploration of energy storage does not end with electricity. Thermal energy storage, harnessing the latent heat of materials to store energy, presents a method to capture and utilize heat from solar collectors or excess electrical energy converted to heat, offering diversification in how energy is stored and used in off-grid settings. This innovation expands the possibilities for heating and cooling solutions, breaking new ground in the quest for a fully sustainable, off-grid existence.

Sustainable Building Materials

At the intersection of architectural ingenuity and environmental stewardship, new materials and building techniques are reimagining the very foundations of off-grid homes. Bio-based materials, such as hempcrete and mycelium composites, emerge as frontrunners, offering not only a reduction in carbon footprint but also superior thermal insulation and moisture regulation properties. These materials, grown and processed with minimal environmental impact, embody the principles of circular economy and sustainability, transforming buildings into entities that breathe with the land rather than impose upon it.

Simultaneously, the advent of 3D printing in construction opens doors to designs that optimize material use and structural integrity while allowing for customization that reflects the individual's connection to their environment. This technology, capable of utilizing local materials to print components on-site, minimizes transportation emissions and waste, further aligning the act of building with the ethos of off-grid living.

In this landscape of emerging technologies in renewable energy, each innovation marks a step forward in the journey toward a sustainable future. Solar power advancements redefine efficiency, and wind and hydropower systems adapt to the nuances of their environments. Energy storage solutions bridge the gap between abundance and need, and sustainable building materials ground homes in the principles of environmental stewardship. Together, they weave a vision of off-grid living not as a compromise but as a celebration of harmony between human ingenuity and the natural world, a testament to the potential that lies in the confluence of innovation and sustainability.

THE GLOBAL OFF-GRID COMMUNITY: CONNECTING WORLDWIDE

In an age where borders blur and distances shrink under the relentless march of digital connectivity, the fabric of the off-grid community stretches beyond local confines, enveloping the globe in a tapestry of shared ideals and mutual aspirations. This network, vast and intricate, thrives on the exchange of knowledge, the celebration of diversity, and the collective pursuit of solutions to the pressing environmental challenges that shadow our planet's future.

International Networks

Within this expansive realm, forums and platforms dedicated to off-grid living have sprouted like mushrooms after rain, each becoming a node in a sprawling web of communication and support. These virtual spaces, alive with the chatter of myriad languages, serve as conduits for the flow of ideas, bridging continents and cultures with the ease of keystrokes. Here, a homesteader in the Scottish Highlands exchanges tips on wind turbine maintenance with a counterpart nestled in the Chilean Andes, while a solar enthusiast in the Sahara shares insights on panel efficiency with a community leader powering a village in the Philippines.

This digital congregation, bound by a shared commitment to sustainable living, transforms individual endeavors into a collective movement, amplifying the impact of localized solutions on a global scale. The diversity of environments and cultures represented within these networks enriches the pool of knowledge, ensuring that innovations born in the peculiarities of one locale find application in the universality of the community's shared goals.

Cultural Exchange

The heart of this global off-grid community beats in rhythm with the cultural exchange that infuses it with vibrancy and depth. Sustainability practices, viewed through the prism of cultural heritage, reveal a spectrum of approaches tailored to the nuances of climate, geography, and tradition. The rainwater harvesting techniques of an indigenous tribe in the Amazon, honed over centuries, offer lessons in efficiency and harmony with nature, while the traditional Japanese concept of Satoyama, living in balance with the forest, provides a model for sustainable land management.

This exchange transcends the mere transfer of knowledge; it fosters mutual respect and appreciation for the richness of cultural diversity and its role in crafting solutions to shared challenges. It underscores the realization that in the quest for sustainability, there are myriad paths, and that wisdom lies in the humility to learn from others, acknowledging that no single culture holds all the answers.

Global Challenges

The call to address the global challenges of climate change, resource depletion, and environmental degradation resonates with urgency within the off-grid community. For those who have chosen a life intertwined with the rhythms of the natural world, these challenges are not abstract threats looming on the horizon but immediate realities that shape their daily existence. As such, the community finds itself on the front lines of innovation, leveraging off-grid living as a laboratory for sustainable practices that mitigate environmental impact.

Projects aimed at carbon sequestration through reforestation, water conservation through intelligent design, and waste reduction through zero-waste living exemplify the proactive stance adopted by off-gridders worldwide. These initiatives, rooted in local action but amplified through the global network, underscore the potential for off-grid living to serve as a blueprint for addressing the environmental crises that confront humanity. By demonstrating that sustainable living is not only viable but desirable, the off-grid community challenges the prevailing paradigms of consumption and waste, advocating for a future where human activity exists in harmony with the planet's ecological boundaries.

Collaborative Projects

The spirit of collaboration, intrinsic to the ethos of off-grid living, finds its fullest expression in projects that span continents and cultures, uniting individuals, and communities in the pursuit of common goals. One such initiative, a global tree-planting endeavor, harnesses the collective power of the off-grid community to combat deforestation and climate change. Participants from every corner of the globe contribute, whether by planting native species in their homesteads or by supporting reforestation efforts in areas ravaged by industrial logging.

Another project, focused on the development of open-source technology for off-grid applications, exemplifies the innovative potential of collaboration. Engineers, designers, and enthusiasts converge on digital platforms to share designs, troubleshoot challenges, and refine solutions that enhance the accessibility and efficiency of off-grid technologies. From solar water heaters fabricated from recycled materials to low-cost wind turbines, these collaborative efforts demystify technology, placing the power of innovation in the hands of the community.

In this intricate dance of connection, exchange, and cooperation, the global off-grid community emerges as a beacon of hope in a world grappling with sustainability challenges. Through the threads of international networks, the richness of cultural exchange, the proactive stance on global issues, and the synergistic potential of collaborative projects, this community transcends geographical and cultural barriers, embodying the principle that unity in diversity can forge a sustainable path forward for humanity. In its collective wisdom and action, the off-grid community offers not just a vision of sustainable living but a testament to the power of global solidarity in crafting solutions for a healthier planet.

ENVIRONMENTAL IMPACT: OFF-GRID LIVING AND GLOBAL SUSTAINABILITY

Within the nuanced tapestry of our planet's ecological narrative, off-grid living emerges not merely as a lifestyle but as an ethos that reverberates with the rhythms of the earth, a harmonious dialogue between humanity and the vast, breathing entity that is our environment. This lifestyle, rooted in the principles of autonomy and interconnectedness, casts ripples across the waters of global sustainability, each wave a testament to the profound impact of individual and collective choices on the health of our planet.

Carbon Footprint Reduction

The pursuit of a life untethered from the grid inherently embodies a commitment to minimizing one's carbon footprint. This commitment transcends the simplicity of reducing energy consumption; it encompasses a holistic approach to living that meticulously considers every aspect of one's ecological impact. From the solar panels that adorn off-grid homes, capturing the sun's bounty to power daily life, to the wood stoves that burn sustainably sourced wood, providing warmth without the reliance on fossil fuels, every element of off-grid living is a carefully chosen thread in the fabric of an environmentally conscious existence.

The cultivation of food within the confines of one's land, a practice embraced with zeal by off-gridders, further exemplifies this commitment. By favoring heirloom seeds and organic methods, off-gridders not only ensure the nutritional richness of their harvest but also fortify the soil, sequestering carbon in its depths. This cycle of growth and renewal, a microcosm of the planet's larger ecological cycles, showcases the potential for human activity to contribute positively to the environment, reversing the narrative of exploitation and degradation that has long dominated our interaction with the earth.

Conservation Efforts

Off-gridders, in their intimate dance with the land, become acutely aware of the fragility and resilience of natural habitats. This awareness, born from daily observation and interaction, fuels a proactive stance toward conservation and a determination to protect and nurture the ecosystems that cradle their way of life. Waterways, forests, meadows, and wetlands, each ecosystem encountered in the realm of off-grid living, is viewed not as a resource to be exploited but as a community of which humans are merely one part.

This perspective drives efforts to restore damaged ecosystems, reintroduce native plants to areas scarred by invasive species, and revitalize streams choked by pollution. The act of planting a tree becomes a declaration of hope, a tangible contribution to the planet's lungs, each sapling a breath of fresh air in the fight against climate change. Through these actions, off-gridders embody the principle that conservation is not a passive endeavor but an active commitment to the stewardship of our planet, a recognition that the health of our environment directly influences the health of humanity.

Sustainable Agriculture

Nestled within the heart of off-grid living lies a vibrant mosaic of sustainable agriculture practices, each plot of land a canvas upon which the principles of permaculture, agroforestry, and biodynamic farming are painted. These practices, diverse in their approaches yet united in their goals, offer a blueprint for agriculture that replenishes rather than depletes and sees the land as a partner in the dance of cultivation rather than a mere backdrop.

By integrating crops with the natural landscape, off-gridders create systems where waste is minimized, biodiversity is celebrated, and the natural pest control and pollination services provided by wildlife are harnessed. This symbiosis, where human activity enriches the ecosystem, showcases the potential for agriculture to exist in harmony with the earth, providing for human needs while fostering the health and diversity of the environment. It is a model that challenges the industrial paradigms of monoculture and chemical dependence, offering a vision of abundance that sustains both the land and those who depend on it.

Water Conservation

The essence of water, vital and fleeting, becomes a focal point in the off-grid ethos, and its conservation reflects the deep respect for this most precious resource. Off-gridders, in their quest to live in balance with the natural world, employ a myriad of strategies to ensure that every drop of water is honored, used with intention, and cherished. Rainwater harvesting systems, simple in concept yet profound in impact, capture the sky's bounty, channeling it to quench gardens, supply households, and replenish aquifers. Greywater systems, innovative in their ability to repurpose water from showers, sinks, and washing machines, transform what was once waste into a resource that nourishes gardens and landscapes.

Beyond the technical, water conservation in off-grid living is imbued with a philosophy that views water not as an unlimited commodity but as a sacred cycle to be preserved and protected. This philosophy guides choices, large and small, from the plants nurtured in the garden, chosen for their drought tolerance, to the mindfulness with which water is used in daily tasks. It is a testament to the belief that with creativity and care, humanity can align its water usage with the rhythms of the natural world, ensuring that rivers continue to flow, lakes remain clear and full, and aquifers are replenished for generations to come.

PREPARING FOR THE FUTURE: OFF-GRID KIDS AND EDUCATION

Raising children within the embrace of an off-grid environment offers a tapestry of experiences markedly distinct from the conventional settings of urban life. In these natural classrooms, young minds absorb lessons from the living world around them, their education seamlessly blending academic learning with practical skills and environmental stewardship. This upbringing, rich in opportunities for hands-on learning and exploration, imbues children with a profound connection to the environment and an intrinsic understanding of sustainability.

Raising Off-Grid Children

In the verdant expanses where off-grid families carve out their existence, children learn from the crackle of firewood, the patterns of weather, and the cycles of plant life. These experiences, though invaluable, come paired with challenges unique to the off grid setting. Access to formal education institutions may be limited, necessitating homeschooling or alternative education strategies that require significant parental involvement and planning. Socialization, too, takes on a different dimension, with fewer peers nearby, pushing parents to seek creative solutions for community engagement. Yet, these hurdles do not detract from the richness of raising children off-grid; rather, they add depth to the experience, fostering in young one's resilience, creativity, and adaptability.

Sustainability Education

Integrating sustainability and environmental education into the learning journey from an early age instills in children an enduring respect for the natural world. This education goes beyond textbook ecology, embedding in daily life through the responsible management of resources, from water conservation practices to the principles of renewable energy. Gardens become classrooms where lessons in biology, chemistry, and economics unfold in the planting and harvesting of crops. Waste management systems teach the importance of reducing, reusing, and recycling, turning theoretical concepts into tangible practices. Through these lived experiences, children grasp the interconnectedness of human actions and environmental health, and their understanding of sustainability is deeply rooted in real-world applications.

Skills for the Future

Equipping children with skills for self-sufficiency and environmental stewardship prepares them not just for off-grid living but for a future where such competencies are increasingly vital. Practical skills such as woodworking, gardening, and animal husbandry meld with softer skills like problem-solving, critical thinking, and cooperation. Digital literacy, too, plays a crucial role, enabling children to navigate the resources and communities available online while maintaining a mindful balance with their natural surroundings. This holistic skill set, combining the traditional with the modern, ensures that off-grid children grow into adults capable of navigating the challenges of their generation with innovation, empathy, and a commitment to sustainability.

Community Involvement

The fabric of off-grid communities, woven from threads of mutual support and shared values, offers a nurturing environment for children to develop a sense of responsibility and belonging. Engaging young ones in community activities, from collective gardening projects to local conservation efforts, fosters a spirit of cooperation and community service. Participation in local decision-making, even in a small capacity, empowers children with a sense of agency and reinforces the importance of active involvement in the collective well-being. These experiences, rich in social interaction and communal learning, cultivate in children an appreciation for the power of community, underscoring the role of collective action in achieving sustainability and resilience.

In this nurturing of off-grid children, where education intertwines with the rhythms of the natural world and the fabric of community life, a blueprint emerges for a future grounded in sustainability, self-sufficiency, and environmental stewardship. This upbringing, marked by challenges transformed into opportunities for growth, equips the next generation with the knowledge, skills, and values needed to navigate an increasingly complex world. Through the integration of sustainability education, the development of practical and future-forward skills, and active involvement in community life, off-grid children become beacons of hope for a sustainable future, their lives a testament to the potential for harmonious coexistence with our planet.

THE LEGACY OF OFF-GRID LIVING: PASSING DOWN KNOWLEDGE

In the quiet solace of the off-grid life, where every action and decision are a stitch in the fabric of self-reliance and sustainability, the act of documenting experiences emerges as a critical thread. This meticulous recording of triumphs and trials serves not merely as a personal ledger but as a beacon for those who will navigate these waters in the future. Diaries brimming with observations on crop rotations that thrived, journals detailing the construction of a rainwater harvesting system, or blogs chronicling the daily rhythms of off-grid life become invaluable resources. They offer a map crafted from the successes and setbacks of those who treaded the path before, ensuring that hard-won wisdom is not lost to the erosion of memory but preserved for the enrichment of future generations.

Mentorship programs within off-grid communities embody the spirit of passing down knowledge and transforming individual expertise into communal wealth. These programs, structured around the sharing of skills and wisdom, foster an environment where learning is reciprocal. Seasoned off-gridders, bearing the knowledge of years shaping life in harmony with the earth, guide newcomers through the intricacies of sustainable living. These relationships, cultivated in the soil of mutual respect and curiosity, ensure that the legacy of off-grid living is not a static relic of the past but a living, breathing tradition that adapts and grows with each new generation.

Creating a legacy of sustainability that extends beyond the confines of individual off-grid communities and influences wider societal values and practices requires a conscious effort. It involves not only the sharing of knowledge and skills but also the embodiment of principles that advocate for a harmonious relationship with the environment. This legacy, woven from the actions, teachings, and ethos of the off-grid community, stands as a testament to the possibility of a sustainable future. It challenges the prevailing narratives of consumption and disposability, offering instead a vision of life that values balance, stewardship, and respect for the natural world. Through this legacy, off-grid living extends its reach, inspiring changes in how wider society interacts with the environment and each other, advocating for a shift toward practices that ensure the well-being of the planet and all its inhabitants.

Encouraging a culture of continued learning and adaptation is the cornerstone upon which the resilience and relevance of off-grid living practices for future generations rest. This culture, nurtured in the fertile ground of curiosity and openness to change, ensures that off-grid living remains a dynamic response to the challenges of sustainability. Workshops exploring new technologies, discussions on adapting traditional methods to modern challenges, and forums debating the best practices for environmental stewardship are just a few examples of how this culture manifests. By fostering an environment where learning is ongoing and adaptation is embraced, off-grid communities ensure that their practices not only survive but thrive, evolving in response to changing environmental conditions and societal needs.

In this manner, the legacy of off-grid living, rooted in the documentation of experiences, the sharing of knowledge through mentorship, the creation of a sustainable heritage, and the cultivation of a culture of continued learning, weaves a rich tapestry. This tapestry, vibrant with the stories, lessons, and principles of those who live in harmony with the earth, offers not just a blueprint for sustainable living but a vision of hope. It speaks to the possibility of a future where humanity thrives, not at the expense of the planet, but in partnership with it, where the legacy of off-grid living illuminates the path toward sustainability and resilience.

As this chapter closes, the essence of off-grid living's legacy shines brightly, a lighthouse guiding toward a sustainable horizon. The meticulous documentation of experiences, nurturing mentorship, the cultivation of a sustainable heritage, and the commitment to perpetual learning together form the bedrock of this legacy. They ensure that the wisdom of living harmoniously with nature is not merely preserved but flourishes, inspiring generations to come. This legacy, rich in knowledge and spirit, seamlessly transitions into the broader dialogue of sustainability, beckoning us forward into a future where balance, respect, and resilience shape our relationship with the planet.

BE AN ADVOCATE FOR SUSTAINABLE LIVING

As you turn the final page of this book, I hope you have already taken all the steps you need to set up your off-grid home in the perfect location. I can imagine you thriving in your new home, tending to your organic garden, and harvesting every drop of water you can. Honing strategies and techniques like aquaponics, food preservation, and setting up solar power will keep you busy in the best way possible, and each one you master will only enhance your sense of self-sufficiency and confidence.

I hope you can take a pause from your busy day to leave a short review. Your words will ensure that other potential off-griders know exactly where they can find the information they need to enjoy the confidence that comes with independence.

WANT TO HELP OTHERS?

Thanks for your support. I wish you much success in your new, autonomous life. Unplugging from the grid is truly the most powerful way to deepen your connection with yourself and the wonder of nature.

Scan the QR code below:

CONCLUSION

As we draw the curtains on this journey, a reflection on the path we've traversed together beckons us to appreciate the transformation that lies at the heart of off-grid living. From the initial steps of embracing an off-grid mindset through the meticulous laying of foundations for self-sufficiency and resilience to mastering the indispensable skills of water purification, food sourcing, and shelter building, this journey has been nothing short of transformative. Together, we've charted a course through the complexities of renewable energy setups and the crafting of sustainable communities, each step echoing the power of independence, sustainability, and a profound reconnection with the natural world.

The essence of our exploration, underscored by the actionable nature of this book, has been to arm you with the knowledge and tools necessary to confidently embark on your off-grid adventure. Remember, the path to off-grid living is paved with practical skills, mental and physical preparation, and the invaluable support of a community that shares your vision and values.

Our collective pursuit of an off-grid lifestyle extends beyond personal fulfillment, contributing to a global movement toward sustainability. By choosing to live off-grid, we not only minimize our carbon footprint but also join a chorus of voices advocating for a more environmentally conscious society. This choice, both bold and beautiful, holds the promise of a future where living in harmony with nature is the norm, not the exception.

I encourage you, dear reader, to take that first decisive step toward your off-grid dream. Whether it's planting the seeds of a garden, harnessing the sun's energy with solar panels, or weaving yourself into the fabric of an off-grid community, each action you take is a building block for a sustainable future. Let us not view off-grid living as a static destination but as a vibrant, evolving journey enriched by continuous learning and the shared wisdom of a supportive community.

Imagine a world where our collective efforts toward off grid living shape a future marked by resilience, independence, and a deep respect for our planet. You, by embracing the principles laid out in this book, are not merely adapting to a lifestyle; you are pioneering a movement that paves the way for generations to come.

Reflecting on my own journey to off-grid living, I'm reminded of the hurdles overcome, the skills honed, and the indescribable fulfillment that comes from a life in sync with the natural rhythms of the earth. It is a path fraught with challenges yet rich with rewards—a testament to the human spirit's resilience and our innate connection to the environment.

As we part ways, I extend my heartfelt gratitude to you for embarking on this exploration with me. Your role in forging a future that values sustainability, resilience, and community cannot be overstated. Together, let us continue to tread lightly on the earth, sharing our stories, learning from each other, and nurturing a legacy of off-grid living that honors the planet and enriches our lives.

Thank you, from the depths of my off-grid heart, for joining me on this journey. May your path be illuminated by the stars above and the earth beneath your feet, guiding you toward a life of profound connection and purpose.

REFERENCES

Bandura, A. (1977). Self-efficacy: Toward a unifying theory of behavioral change. *Journal of Personality and Social Psychology, 34*(2), 191-215. https://doi.org/10. 1037/0022-3514.34.2.191

Sankofa, C. (n.d.). 50 off the grid quotes for living free. *Everyday Power*. Retrieved from https://everydaypower.com/off-the-grid-quotes/

SFC Energy. (2024, April 2). Off grid energy. Retrieved from https://www.sfc.com/ en/glossar/off-grid-energy/

Be Ready Utah. (n.d.). Signaling. Retrieved from https://beready.utah.gov/family-preparedness/12-areas-of-preparedness/communication/signaling/

Building Performance. (2023, August 9). Using thermal mass for heating and cooling. Retrieved from https://www.building.govt.nz/getting-started/smarter-homes-guides/design/using-thermal-mass-for-heating-and-cooling/

Center for American Progress. (2008, April 16). It's easy being green: Living off the grid. Retrieved from https://www.americanprogress.org/article/its-easy-being-green-living-off-the-grid/

Christa. (2020, April 1). How to watch wildlife ethically. *Expedition Wildlife*. Retrieved from https://www.expeditionwildlife.com/how-to-watch-wildlife-ethically/

Cuffari, B. (2020, December 1). Farm from a box: Off-grid toolkits for sustainable agriculture. *AZoCleantech*. Retrieved from https://www.azocleantech.com/ article.aspx?ArticleID=1159

Discover Real Food in Texas. (n.d.). Off the grid living: Natural home building techniques and tips. Retrieved from https://discover.texasrealfood.com/off-grid-living/natural-home-building

Energy.gov. (n.d.). Off-grid or stand-alone renewable energy systems. Retrieved from https://www.energy.gov/energysaver/grid-or-stand-alone-renewable-energy-systems

Gilbert, S. (2019, November 18). The importance of community and mental health. *National Alliance on Mental Illness*. Retrieved from https://www.nami.org/Blogs/ NAMI-Blog/November-2019/The-Importance-of-Community-and-Mental-Health

Glines, A. (2024, February 14). Legal considerations and zoning laws for off-grid living. *Medium*. Retrieved from https://imallenglines.medium.com/legal-considerations-and-zoning-laws-for-off-grid-living-7505443039a7

GoGreenSolar.com. (n.d.). DIY solar panel installation: Step by step guide. Retrieved from https://www.gogreensolar.com/pages/diy-solar-installation-guide

GORE-TEX. (2017, November 8). Foraging for beginners: Tips for safely gathering wild, edible foods. Retrieved from https://www.gore-tex.com/blog/foraging-food-wild-plants

Grayson, R. (2022, August 18). 6. Pioneers of the off-grid. *Pacific Edge*. Retrieved from https://medium.com/pacificedge/6-pioneers-of-the-off-grid-6d7053793384

Growatt. (2024, February 27). Growatt. Retrieved from https://growattportable.com/blogs/news/5-best-states-to-live-off-grid

Hamilton, J. (2020, December 22). The link between self-sufficiency & mental health. *Australian & New Zealand Mental Health Association*. Retrieved from https://anzmh.asn.au/blog/mental-health/link-self-sufficiency-mental-health

Jordan, A. (2023, November 21). 15 ways to live off the grid. *WikiHow*. Retrieved from https://www.wikihow.com/Live-off-the-Grid

Keys, S. (2019, June 14). Why is off-grid living good for your mental health? *Real Goods*. Retrieved from https://realgoods.com/blog/why-is-off-grid-living-good-for-your-mental-health/

Kirkland, E. (2015, September 9). Forest schools: Education in the great outdoors. *Outdoor Families Magazine*. Retrieved from https://outdoorfamiliesonline.com/forest-schools-education-in-the-great-outdoors/

Levi, J. (2023, July 6). Wildlife conservation through hunting: A sustainable approach. *Ambush Hunting Blinds*. Retrieved from https://ambushhuntingblinds.com/wildlife-conservation-through-hunting/

Loper, S. A. (2015, June). PNNL-24347 rainwater harvesting state regulations and technical resources. *Pacific Northwest National Laboratory*. Retrieved from https://www.pnnl.gov/main/publications/external/technical_reports/PNNL-24347.pdf

Mack, E. (2023, September 7). Living off-grid comes with both savings and hidden expenses. *CNET*. Retrieved from https://www.cnet.com/home/energy-and-utilities/living-off-grid-comes-with-both-savings-and-hidden-expenses/

MacWelch, T. (2019, October 3). Survival skills: 10 ways to purify water. *Outdoor Life*. Retrieved from https://www.outdoorlife.com/survival-skills-ways-to-purify-water/

mdavis19. (n.d.). How I built an electricity producing wind turbine. *Instructables*. Retrieved from https://www.instructables.com/How-I-built-an-electricity-producing-wind-turbine/

NFPA. (n.d.). Preparing homes for wildfire. Retrieved from https://www.nfpa.org/education-and-research/wildfire/preparing-homes-for-wildfire

REI Co-op. (n.d.-a). How to read a topo map. Retrieved from https://www.rei.com/learn/expert-advice/topo-maps-how-to-use.html

REI Co-op. (n.d.-b). Wilderness first aid basics. Retrieved from https://www.rei.com/learn/expert-advice/wilderness-first-aid-basics.html

Richardson, A. (2023, January). How you can design your home to be more sustainable. *Simple Dwelling*. Retrieved from https://simpledwelling.net/episodes/design-principles/5-principles-for-sustainable-home-design

Silverstein, K. (2023, October 10). If this technology breaks through, solar energy will skyrocket. *Forbes*. Retrieved from https://www.forbes.com/sites/kensilverstein/2023/10/10/if-this-technology-breaks-through-solar-energy-will-skyrocket/

Smeele, I. (2016). Advice for creating an off-grid sustainable community. (Ecovillage Forum at Permies). *Permies.com*. Retrieved from https://www.permies.com/t/52186/Advice-creating-grid-sustainable-community

Sweetser, R. (2024, January 10). Organic gardening basics: How to start an organic garden. *Almanac.com*. Retrieved from https://www.almanac.com/organic-gardening-basics-how-start-organic-garden

UGREEN. (2023, September 15). The 21 best off-grid communities in the world, there's one for you. Retrieved from https://www.ugreen.com/blogs/off-grid-living/best-off-grid-communities-in-the-world

Wichelns, R. (2023, May 23). The 9 best hiking GPS devices. *Popular Mechanics*. Retrieved from https://www.popularmechanics.com/adventure/outdoor-gear/g38442114/best-hiking-gps/

www.ingramcontent.com/pod-product-compliance
Lightning Source LLC
Chambersburg PA
CBHW032055040426
42335CB00037B/719